Aldeburgh Poetry Festival Anthology 1989 – 1998

EDITED BY

Roy Blackman

Michael Laskey

The Aldeburgh Poetry Trust

Published 1999 by the Aldeburgh Poetry Trust
Goldings, Goldings Lane, Leiston, Suffolk IP16 4EB

ISBN 0 9535422 1 1

Typeset at Reading Room Yard, Brockdish

Printed in Great Britain by Thorndick & Dawson Ltd, Norwich

SUPPORTED BY
THE NATIONAL LOTTERY
THROUGH
THE ARTS COUNCIL
OF ENGLAND

Aldeburgh Poetry Festival Anthology 1989 – 1998

EDITED BY

Roy Blackman

Michael Laskey

The Aldeburgh Poetry Trust

Published 1999 by the Aldeburgh Poetry Trust
Goldings, Goldings Lane, Leiston, Suffolk IP16 4EB

ISBN 0 9535422 1 1

Typeset at Reading Room Yard, Brockdish

Printed in Great Britain by Thorndick & Dawson Ltd, Norwich

SUPPORTED BY
THE NATIONAL LOTTERY
THROUGH
THE ARTS COUNCIL
OF ENGLAND

Introduction

The Aldeburgh Poetry Festival, taking place annually over the first weekend in November, has played a significant part over the last decade in bringing contemporary poetry to a wider public. Audiences even at the first Festival in 1989 averaged an impressive eighty for each event and they've continued to grow steadily till they now consistently top two hundred.

How does one account for this success? Certainly the place itself with its rich cultural associations and its many attractions and amenities as a small seaside town has been a huge bonus. But in our view it's the guiding principles behind the programming that have given this Aldeburgh experience its unique appeal. Over its first ten years the Festival has grown and developed – incorporating workshops, events for children, a masterclass, film, a thriving fringe, writers-in-residence and a pre-festival tour – but its core has remained unchanged. Without fail this has consisted of four three-handed readings; a small press or magazine event; and a late-night cabaret-type performance. The emphasis has always been on readings: contemporary poets delivering their own work. And the poets – regional, national and international – never the same: a different set invited every year.

In Britain these have been times of increasing plurality for poetry and the Festival has always celebrated its quality and range. No longer dominated by a handful of white, male, Oxbridge-educated, London-based poets, contemporary writing is well served by a network of regional publishers and non-metropolitan magazines. The nurturing work of the Arvon Foundation and the expanding demand for degree-level writing courses is clear evidence of an increasing democratisation. Women have come into their own. Regional accents abound. Ireland's ever strong sense of poetic identity is matched these days in Scotland and Wales. Gifted young black British writers now have a real choice of role models. And in the last ten years performance poetry has gone into orbit. So many poets worth listening to.

In putting together this anthology to chronicle the Festival's first decade, our aim has been to represent our one hundred and seventy-six poets by one poem each, for preference one they actually read in Aldeburgh. When we had doubts we consulted the poets, and if they couldn't help we've chosen a poem of the right vintage which we admire.

The policy of always inviting different poets has occasionally been breached. From 1990 on, the Festival has opened with a reading for children, so several sections in the book begin with a poem for children. But sometimes the children's poet has appeared in the same or a different year reading to the adult audience – Jackie Kay, Adrian Mitchell, Brian Patten, Matthew Sweeney and Kit Wright – and we've chosen to represent them by their adult poems. Poets like Michael Hamburger and Frances Wilson took part in magazine readings and later appeared in their own right. Donald Atkinson read first for Ambit and promptly returned the next year as the winner of the Festival first collection prize. Kathleen Jamie gave a memorable late-night performance with Andrew Greig of their jointly-written *A Flame in Your Heart* and came again solo in 1998. We've arranged the poets by year and generally followed the order in which they read. This means that you can sample the unique narrative of each Festival.

Reading styles vary, but invariably the poem gains an added dimension when we hear the poet reading it. It's not just that the poet's introduction – the intention, some background detail, a clarification of an obscurity, an anecdote – can allow us to enter the poem more fully. But poetry is pre-eminently, in Auden's phrase, memorable speech, and the poem is written for the poet's voice – its tone, its timbre, its turns of phrase – and so that intimate connection between the written and the spoken word is always illuminating. We're grateful to have been reminded of the vitality and individuality of all these voices. And confident too that you'll enjoy them and share, with the loyal Aldeburgh audiences, the pleasure of discovering fine poems by poets both well-known and new to you.

Roy Blackman & Michael Laskey
Suffolk 1999

Contents

1989

The Skip *James Fenton* 3
Apple Pie in Pizzaland *Maura Dooley* 5
My Father Fading Out *Ken Smith* 6
Reading Pascal in the Lowlands *Douglas Dunn* 7
Eldon Hole *David Constantine* 9
Broken Moon *Carole Satyamurti* 10
The Sea *E. A. Markham* 11
from: Advertisement for Itself *Sebastian Barker* 12
Love Song of the Thracian Horseman *Anne Beresford* 13
Poor Moorhen Johnny *Terrence Hirst* 14
Midnight Garden *Michael Mackmin* 15
Road Through Northern Landscape *Hilary Mellon* 16
The Dig *Pauline Stainer* 17
A Sea Family *John Wakeman* 18
Wednesday *John Fuller* 19
A Prayer to Live with Real People *Anne Stevenson* 20
The Butchers *Michael Longley* 21
On the Beach at Thorpeness *Michael Hofmann* 22
Neighbours *Gillian Clarke* 23
The First Men on Mercury *Edwin Morgan* 24

1990

Scary Monsters *Mick Gowar* 29
All Legendary Obstacles *John Montague* 31
Make Believe *Gerda Mayer* 32
Dolphins *Stephen Spender* 33
Catching Crabs *David Dabydeen* 34
Translating the English, 1989 *Carol Ann Duffy* 35
Sea Lady *Herbert Lomas* 36
Says the Southerner *Judi Benson* 38
Mourning *Judy Gahagan* 39
Phil's Poem *Martin Stannard* 40
Studying Grosz on the Bus *John Lucas* 41
A Picture of My Parents with their First Television *George Szirtes* 42
The Fox Gallery *Charles Tomlinson* 43
from: A Flame in Your Heart *Andrew Greig* 44
Omens *Marin Sorescu* 45
My Mother's Lips *C. K. Williams* 46
Brief Reflection on Cats Growing in Trees *Miroslav Holub* 48

1991

Wailing Begins at the House-Wall *Donald Atkinson* 53
from: The Adoption Papers *Jackie Kay* 55
The Automatic Days *Alan Brownjohn* 56
Roadworkers Picking Cherries *Michael Hulse* 57
Soup *Tony Curtis* 58
From Lucy: A Favour *James Berry* 59
Cutting Loose *Liz Cashdan* 60
Fifty Years On *Janet Fisher* 61
Geography Lesson *Christine McNeill* 62
Sacrificial Wolf *Anne Rouse* 63
from: A Meeting of Innocents: A Birthday Sequence *Carol Rumens* 64
In a Country Museum *Patricia Beer* 65
Eden Rock *Charles Causley* 66
Underneath the Archers *Kit Wright* 67
On the Way to Heaven *Joan Jobe Smith* 70
Variations on a Theme by William Carlos Williams *Kenneth Koch* 72
Fish *Adam Czerniawski* 73
Uptight *Fred Voss* 74
Temptation *Nina Cassian* 75

1992

Alice and Alice *John Mole* 79
Cleaning Ladies *Mark Roper* 81
A Friendship *Connie Bensley* 82
HMS Glasshouse *Sean O'Brien* 83
Summer Pudding *Grevel Lindop* 85
A Noted Judge of Horses *Bernard O'Donoghue* 87
An Innocent Adultery *Sylvia Kantaris* 88
Indian Cooking *Moniza Alvi* 89
The Bottom Back Nut *Duncan Curry* 90
Nobel Prize Poem *Geoff Hattersley* 91
One Day, Her Father *Jeanette Hattersley* 92
Crossing Point *Myra Schneider* 93
Change of State *John Latham* 95
The Kiss *Brendan Kennelly* 96
Scrubbing the Furious Walls of Mikuyu *Jack Mapanje* 98
Love in a Bathtub *Sujata Bhatt* 99
In Doubt *Michael Hamburger* 100
Going Westwards *Sorley MacLean* 101

1993

Jumping Jack *Wes Magee* 105
Branches *Susan Wicks* 106
Goat *Jo Shapcott* 107
A Classroom *Elizabeth Jennings* 108
The Duke of Nowhere *Philip Gross* 109
The Last Wolf in Scotland *Sheenagh Pugh* 111
Playing For England *David Scott* 112
This Poem... *Elma Mitchell* 114
Rafaela Padilla *Julio Valle-Castillo* 115
Going out: Lancasters, 1944 *Peter Scupham* 116
Places We Love *Ivan V. Lalíc* 117
Names *Wendy Cope* 118
Way of Life *Dennis O'Driscoll* 119
Report on an Angel *Vyacheslav Kupriyanov* 120
That Island Formed You *Iain Crichton Smith* 121

1994

Hot Food *Michael Rosen* 125
Asleep in a Chair *Matthew Sweeney* 126
Tango *Meg Peacocke* 127
Palm Tree King *John Agard* 128
A Dream Mistaking a Person for What He Has Come to Represent *Peter Sansom* 130
The Doctor Book *Donna Hilbert* 131
The Myth of the Twin *John Burnside* 132
Lily Pond *Vicki Feaver* 133
Some Notes About a Hare *Robert Etty* 134
Chet Baker *John Harvey* 135
The Boston School of Cooking Cookbook *Rhona McAdam* 136
In the Chelsea Physic Garden *Tamar Yoseloff* 137
The Ferryman's Arms *Don Paterson* 138
The Island *Selima Hill* 139
Waiting-Room *Zsuzsa Rakovszky* 140
Cinders *Roger McGough* 142
from: Last Eternal Moments *Frank Kuppner* 143
The Valley *Rutger Kopland* 144
Planting a Sequoia *Dana Gioia* 145

1995

from: Unrelated Incidents *Tom Leonard* 149
Bluebells *Sue Stewart* 150
After the Deafening *Gerard Woodward* 151
Hymns Ancient and Modern *Lauris Edmond* 152
Two Boyfriends *Norman Silver* 154
Moggy at Grimma's *Dorothy Nimmo* 155
Castration *Nigel Jenkins* 156
Breaking Siesta *John Lyons* 158
Lovesong to Captain James T. Kirk *Deryn Rees-Jones* 159
Crawley Welcomes Careful Drivers *Charles Boyle* 161
Two Family Snaps *Peter Bland* 162
From the Irish *Ian Duhig* 163
The Wonders of the World *Grete Tartler* 164
News from Gloucestershire *P. J. Kavanagh* 165
A Puppy Called Puberty *Adrian Mitchell* 166
Would You Jump Into My Grave As Quick? *Paula Meehan* 167
from: The Eighth Day of the Week *Eira Stenberg* 168
Skating with Heather Grace *Thomas Lynch* 169

1996

Flowers in the Kitchen *Lemn Sissay* 173
The Language Issue *Nuala Ní Dhomhnaill* 174
The Tattoo *Peter Finch* 175
The Surf Motel *Stephen Knight* 176
Against Coupling *Fleur Adcock* 177
Life *Patricia Pogson* 178
When I Grow Up *Hugo Williams* 179
The Stars *Duncan Forbes* 181
Braided Rug *Jane Duran* 182
from: Six Poems on Nothing *Gwyneth Lewis* 183
Popular Mechanics *Charles Simic* 185
Right Dress *Vernon Scannell* 186
A Blade of Grass *Brian Patten* 187
Alba Einstein *Robert Crawford* 188
The Blue Dress *Sharon Olds* 189
Busy with Many Jobs *Tadeusz Różewicz* 191

1997

Knowing Plenty *Glyn Wright* 195
Living in Real Times *Duncan Bush* 197
Spring Cleaning *Jean 'Binta' Breeze* 199
The Innocence of Radium *Lavinia Greenlaw* 202
The Elocution Lesson *Ruth Silcock* 204
Cockroach Story *Anthony Thwaite* 205
A Manager Writes *Jonathan Davidson* 207
Counting *Jackie Wills* 209
The Silo *John Kinsella* 210
Walking With My Father *Jim Burns* 211
'I love all things in miniature' *Mimi Khalvati* 212
How to Like It *Stephen Dobyns* 213
Kidspoem/Bairnsang *Liz Lochhead* 215
That Summer *Eiléan Ní Chuilleanáin* 216
'Death does not come from outside' *Jaan Kaplinski* 217
It Allows a Portrait in Line Scan at Fifteen *Les Murray* 218

1998

Some Tentative Definitions I *Kwame Dawes* 223
St Bride's *Kathleen Jamie* 224
The Shout *Simon Armitage* 225
The Marble Fly *Jamie McKendrick* 226
Three Ways of Recovering a Body *Helen Dunmore* 227
from: New Numbers *Christopher Logue* 229
The Creation *Allan E. Baker* 231
Deadnettle *Jean Sprackland* 232
Changes *John Lynch* 233
Revisiting the Pigs *Frances Wilson* 234
Translation Workshop: Grit and Blood *Kevin Crossley-Holland* 235
The Did-You-Come-Yets of the Western World *Rita Ann Higgins* 236
An Interrupted Letter *Dannie Abse* 238
Ticket to Staines *Sophie Hannah* 239
from: Project *M. C. Jabber* 240
Watching Young Couples with an Old Girlfriend on Sunday Morning *August Kleinzahler* 241
Hurricane Story, 1988 *Olive Senior* 242
Evening *Shuntarō Tanikawa* 243

Acknowledgements 245

The First
Aldeburgh Poetry Festival
10 – 12 November 1989

A Sense of Place

Sebastian Barker
Anne Beresford
Gillian Clarke
David Constantine
Maura Dooley
Douglas Dunn
James Fenton
John Fuller
Terrence Hirst
Michael Hofmann
Michael Longley
Michael Mackmin
E. A. Markham
Hilary Mellon
Edwin Morgan
Carole Satyamurti
Ken Smith
Pauline Stainer
Anne Stevenson
John Wakeman

The Skip

I took my life and threw it on the skip,
Reckoning the next-door neighbours wouldn't mind
If my life hitched a lift to the council tip
With their dry rot and rubble. What you find

With skips is – the whole community joins in.
Old mattresses appear, doors kind of drift
Along with all that won't fit in the bin
And what the bin-men can't be fished to shift.

I threw away my life, and there it lay
And grew quite sodden. 'What a dreadful shame,'
Clucked some old bag and sucked her teeth: 'The way
The young these days... no values... me, I blame...'

But I blamed no one. Quality control
Had loused it up, and that was that. 'Nough said.
I couldn't stick at home. I took a stroll
And passed the skip, and left my life for dead.

Without my life, the beer was just as foul,
The landlord still as filthy as his wife,
The chicken in the basket was an owl,
And no one said: 'Ee, Jim-lad, whur's thee life?'

Well, I got back that night the worse for wear,
But still just capable of single vision;
Looked in the skip; my life – it wasn't there!
Some bugger'd nicked it – *without* my permission.

Okay, so I got angry and began
To shout, and woke the street. Okay. *Okay!*
And I was sick all down the neighbour's van.
And I disgraced myself on the par-*kay*.

And then...you know how if you've had a few
You'll wake at dawn, all healthy, like sea breezes,

Raring to go, and thinking: 'Clever you!
You've got away with it.' And then, oh Jesus,

It hits you. Well, that morning, just at six
I woke, got up and looked down at the skip.
There lay my life, still sodden, on the bricks;
There lay my poor old life, arse over tip.

Or was it mine? Still dressed, I went downstairs
And took a long cool look. The truth was dawning.
Someone had just exchanged my life for theirs.
Poor fool, I thought – I should have left a warning.

Some bastard saw my life and thought it nicer
Than what he had. Yet what he'd had seemed fine.
He'd never caught his fingers in the slicer
The way I'd managed in that life of mine.

His life lay glistening in the rain, neglected,
Yet still a decent, an authentic life.
Some people I can think of, I reflected
Would take that thing as soon as you'd say Knife.

It seemed a shame to miss a chance like that.
I brought the life in, dried it by the stove.
It looked so fetching, stretched out on the mat.
I tried it on. It fitted, like a glove.

And now, when some local bat drops off the twig
And new folk take the house, and pull up floors
And knock down walls and hire some kind of big
Container (say, a skip) for their old doors,

I'll watch it like a hawk, and every day
I'll make at least – oh – half a dozen trips.
I've furnished an existence in that way.
You'd not believe the things you find on skips.

James Fenton

Apple Pie in Pizzaland

We are apologising to one another
for our shynesses. The waitress apologises
for the lack of sultanas (not like the picture,
she says). I still probe between the slices of
apple as if I expect to find something other than
air. You spin the menu and pleat the paper napkin,
our cutlery scrapes eloquently enough.

On the train here a Canadian told me how
his province holds a lake the size of England.
I imagine you and I and Pizzaland, the green tables,
Doncaster, the fields, motorways, castles and flats,
churches, factories, corner shops, pylons, Hinkley Point,
Lands End and all of us dropped
in that huge lake, *plop*.

Years later new people will stroll on
the banks, remarking how in drought
you might see the top of Centrepoint
and in the strange stillness hear the ghostly
ring and clatter of Pizzaland forks on plates.

Maura Dooley

My Father Fading Out

Each time I recall him he's grown
thinner and paler, *am I*
making myself clear he shouts
from the hearthstone, already

I see almost through him
asleep at the fire, exhausted
evening by evening, his crossed feet
pink and opaque at the open oven door.

If he slams out now it will be
fainter and shake the house less,
less curl to his lip for his bosses –
Reggie Rat, Charlie Woods, Wallace Dixon.

For them he went topping and tailing
bent through the frozen turnips,
or stooking in summer pitched his fork
high in the air in blind sudden anger.

Now he fades out, the wireless
plays him to sleep, he wakes, asks news,
sees in the coals the black flag of a stranger,
dozes again, then is gone completely.

Ken Smith

Reading Pascal in the Lowlands

His aunt has gone astray in her concern
And the boy's mum leans across his wheelchair
To talk to him. She points to the river.
An aged angler and a boy they know
Cast lazily into the rippled sun.
They go there, into the dappled grass, shadows
Bickering and falling from the shaken leaves.

His father keeps apart from them, walking
On the beautiful grass that is bright green
In the sunlight of July at 7 p.m.
He sits on the bench beside me, saying
It is a lovely evening, and I rise
From my sorrows, agreeing with him.
His large hand picks tobacco from a tin;

His smile falls at my feet, on the baked earth
Shoes have shuffled over and ungrassed.
It is discourteous to ask about
Accidents, or of the sick, the unfortunate.
I do not need to, for he says 'Leukaemia'.
We look at the river, his son holding a rod,
The line going downstream in a cloud of flies.

I close my book, the *Pensée*s of Pascal.
I am light with meditation, religiose
And mystic with a day of solitude.
I do not tell him of my own sorrows.
He is bored with misery and premonition.
He has seen the limits of time, asking 'Why?'
Nature is silent on that question.

A swing squeaks in the distance. Runners jog
Round the perimeter. He is indiscreet.
His son is eight years old, with months to live.
His right hand trembles on his cigarette.
He sees my book, and then he looks at me,
Knowing me for a stranger. I have said
I am sorry. What more is there to say?

He is called over to the riverbank.
I go away, leaving the Park, walking through
The Golf Course, and then a wood, climbing,
And then bracken and gorse, sheep pasturage.
From a panoptic hill I look down on
A little town, its estuary, its bridge,
Its houses, churches, its undramatic streets.

Douglas Dunn

Eldon Hole

They fastened a poor man here on a rope's end
And through the turbulence of the jackdaws let him down
To where everything lost collects, all the earth's cold,
And the crying of fallen things goes round and round
And where, if anywhere, the worm is coiled.

When he had filled with cold they hauled him up.
The horrors were swarming in his beard and hair.
His teeth had broken chattering and could not stop
Mincing his tongue. He lay in the rope and stared,
Stared at the sky and feared he would live for ever.

Like one of those dreadful fish that are all head
They saw him at his little window beaming out
Bald and whiskerless and squiddy-eyed
He hung in the branches of their nightmares like a swede.
They listened at his door for in his throat

Poor Isaac when the wounds in his mouth had healed
Talked to himself deep down. It was a sound
Like the never-ending yelps of a small stone
Falling to where the worm lives and the cold
And everything hurt goes round and round and round.

David Constantine

Broken Moon

Twelve, small as six,
strength, movement, hearing
all given in half measure,
my daughter,
child of genetic carelessness,
walks uphill, always.

I watch her morning face;
precocious patience as she hooks each sock,
creeps it up her foot,
aims her jersey like a quoit.
My fingers twitch;
her private frown deters.

Her jokes can sting:
'My life is like dressed crab
– lot of effort, rather little meat.'
Yet she delights in seedlings taking root,
finding a fossil,
a surprise dessert.

Chopin will not yield to her stiff touch;
I hear her cursing.
She paces Bach exactly,
firm rounding of perfect cadences.
Somewhere inside
she is dancing a courante.

In dreams she skims the sand,
curls toes into the ooze of pools,
leaps on to stanchions.
Awake, her cousins take her hands;
they lean into the waves,
stick-child between curved sturdiness.

She turns away from stares,
laughs at the boy who asks
if she will find a midget husband.
Ten years ago, cradling her,
I showed her the slice of silver in the sky.
'Moon broken', she said.

Carole Satyamurti

The Sea

It used to be at the bottom of the hill
and brought white ships and news
of a far land where half my life
was scheduled to be lived.

That was at least half a life ago
of managing without maps, plans, permanence
of a dozen or more addresses
of riding the trains like a vagrant.

Today, I have visitors. They come
long distances overland. They will be uneasy
and console me for loss of the sea.
I will discourage them.

E. A. Markham

from: ADVERTISEMENT FOR ITSELF

To intend to write poems is, of course, the first way to fail.
If, however, you don't intend to write them
They never get written. In that case, you may well ask,
How did they get written? The answer to this is quite simple.
They write themselves. Poems are so clever, you see,
They are able to do this. They can also roll on their backs
Laughing at pompous asses. Or get down on their knees
And scrub the kitchen floor the guests have trampled on
All night, swirling martinis, stubbing their butts in the breadbin.
Nothing is impossible to the poem. The trickiest problems –
Like how to fix the jets of a Solex carburettor
Or the world's moral impasse – to it are kid's stuff.
Trees crack and fall, the nests of crows explode
In horrible gales, but the poem, like the burning hoop,
To the lion roaring through it, remains unmoved.
Small ants hide in the shadow of a trouserleg
Clutching their silly pieces of wood, but our bold hero's
Like Jack and the Beanstalk. A poem knows no limits.
This is not because it is stupid, but because
It cannot understand the elementary paradox
Of a limited universe. It resembles the scientist,
Philosopher or logician. But unlike each of these
It cannot understand its own explications
Even long enough to hear them out. It is, in fact,
Pure ignorance masquerading as scripture – which obviously it
can't be
Since this is the Word of God. It is, then,
The old voice, fresher than lilies, discoursing
To another, just the same. It's so new, I do believe,
Photographs only expose the last age of countless.
Critics, too, are baffled by why their own brains
Seem more the object of study than the subject in hand.
The poem, therefore, returns them every sympathy.

Sebastian Barker

Love Song of the Thracian Horseman

I will throw you
only the chicken breast
and the largest crusts
from the whitest bread

You shall drink the best
wine from my cup
your lips on
the imprint of mine

I will give you
seventeen gold beads
each one a flower
on a gold chain

I will give you
some bracelets
yellow snakes to coil
lovingly over your arms

I will hand you
my sharpest spear
that you may impale me
on our love

You are my wild
golden maned horse
I shall gallop you
miles into the night

Anne Beresford

Poor Moorhen Johnny

Last call today on Poor Moorhen Johnny
Who kept the sluice by the lower water meadow.
Trusted by otters, counting marsh harriers
Among close friends.

Taught me wildfowling with a punt gun
His grandfather made.
Long birdlike fingers sharing a sandwich
In the bottom of a flat-sided skiff,
Slyly rolling Sun Valley in rice paper
But never smoking lest it frighten the duck.

Poor Moorhen Johnny who blew out his brains
With that same twelve bore
I carried from Aldeby to Burgh St. Peter
On sharp sugar beet walking mornings.

George Aldous, son of two centuries of marsh farmers,
Says there'll be no funeral,
Just a burying.

Splinters of his skull hanging from the hawthorn
About his home,
Bleeding icicles.
A single room of shabby books, books of birds,
Photographs of a trip to Norwich.

'Thank you Doctor, for all you done'.

A jay flew so close to the windscreen
Yesterday on the old station road
Poor Moorhen Johnny.
'You couldn't have done nothing, sir,
Thanks for all you done'.

Terrence Hirst

Midnight Garden

As the light moves from deepest blue to black
among the last outlines of vines and roses the white
planes of the painted table top and seats of chairs
slide into that mist where sight and insight wait
the last green flare, phenomenal illumination,
and eyes begin to blur, catching in corners at
the ghosts of rats, auras of uncertainties,
as if and where the lamp of Vichy shines
and the worn cards in their grey gloss fix in the hands.

And then the night: the labouring bee is frozen
on the stem of thyme, the recollections of geranium,
the different reds and white, fitting to those ancient
landscapes of the heart, the voices of sheep
hooves banging on soft stone, all gone dark, obscure,
reliant on memory – the eyes' pulse
pulling at afterglow, the least glitter, seeing
the sound of the dead wind the tired dry
iron wheels on iron rails, wheels on rails, rails.

Michael Mackmin

Road Through Northern Landscape

The town rewinds its streets and blackened mills,
an urban landscape lost before it's seen.
The road unrolls across a line of hills
exposing fields with thirteen shades of green.
The valley slips and stumbles out of sight
where sheep are fixed at angles to the ground,
tall trees colliding blindly with the light
while jutted rocks point scornfully around.

Another town is hit, its public face:
the dark canal all choked with plastic trash,
a dirty terrace viewed through pristine lace
as fists of sunlight break the window sash.
Then on again, the road: its edges sewn
where ragged sheets of moor are ripped by stone.

Hilary Mellon

The Dig

They map out the mound
like surgeons
dividing a belly,
scan for echoes.

Here the stern
of the burial-boat
was removed by ploughing.

On this female grave,
they uncover the goosewing
with which she swept out the oven;
the worn spiral
of an ammonite
where her dress
once opened at the breast.

It is quirkish of time
to leave only a purposeful echo
among the erratics:

this male body
buried in ploughing-position
beside his plough,
the eager figure
bent forward over the coulter –
fragile, passionate,
as if still reining-in
the light.

Pauline Stainer

A Sea Family

A still-born boy is wrapped
in clean matting
and the Niger takes him gently
to the sea and an old drunk
kicked to death in Glasgow his broken face
veined like the map of Skye where he was born
makes his way out through the Firth of Clyde
submerged to avoid interfering policemen
and out and out sneaking past Ireland
to the sea which was always in his alcoholic blood
and a girl in a village near Lisbon
passes the white sailors' church
forgetting the fat postman who took her
once to the movies and never dared again
so she steps at dawn into the pearly sea
believing no one has ever loved her
and the old man hugs the baby
to his smashed ribs and the girl
holds them safe in her flayed arms
and they converse together
and stroll with the tides and the turning moon
amazed at the bright ships, the great fishes.

John Wakeman

Erratum

John Fuller's poem Wednesday
should have continued over the page as follows:

And when you were found, a stretched effigy,
A hard object so much like yourself
   But weirdly without motion
   And feared like an impostor,

The ensuing sorrow was the strangest thing,
A conscious grieving in a larger happiness
   That seemed designed to absorb
   Its choking negative.

Whatever strange lessons of death we learned
Touching your flat still body or pushing turf
   Into impromptu place
   Above the disturbed earth,

We prefer to make of you a remembered image
That accords with our myth of perpetual contentment,
   Of life as an unfolding
   Towards an unseen horizon.

And now at evening in the summer air,
With wine and fruit unfinished on the table,
   The candle sculpts a soft
   But meagre circle of shadows.

And as night comes, the garden is suddenly empty
Of a black shape in the blackness, coming from nowhere,
   Coming at an idle call
   Though never making a sound.

John Fuller

Wednesday

Wednesday, black rabbit, seven years old,
You were silent all your short life as though
  Entrusted with a secret
  You could not be sure of keeping.

Easily startled, you would never turn your head
But stared in a still alarm through creepered brick
  Into that missing meadow
  Where danger would be a delight.

Not the eyes, a cloudy lidless brown,
But scissored ears positioned like microphones
  Brought the imaginary
  Misty horizons near.

Sometimes you dashed in joy from bed to bed
Like a comedian with surprises in the wings,
  Feet avoiding the fronds
  With a fastidious flick.

Not so many abortive burrows were yours
But the same one, not serious, under the rose.
  Your preferred occupations
  Were transporting paper

Or making circles around our wary heels
When on dewy evenings we trod
  With purpose or excuse
  Into your green domain.

Sturdy little president of the lawn!
We ignored your private moods; your gaiety
  Was at most a flourish
  In our casual moments.

John Fuller

A Prayer to Live with Real People

Let me not live, ever, without fat people,
the marshmallow flesh set thick on the muscular bone,
the silk white perms of sweet sixteen-stone ladies,
luscious as pom-poms or full blown perfumed magnolias,
with breasts like cottage loaves dropped into lace-knit sweaters,
all cream-bun arms and bottoms in sticky leathers.
O Russian dolls, o range of hills
rosy behind the glo-green park of the pool table,
thorns are not neater or sharper than your delicate shoes.

Let me not live, ever, without pub people,
the tattooed forearm steering the cue like a pencil,
the twelve-pint belly who adds up the scores in his head,
the wiry owner of whippets, the keeper of ferrets,
thin wives who suffer, who are silent, who talk with their eyes,
the girl who's discovered that sex is for she who tries.
o zebra blouse, o vampish back
blown like a lily from the swaying stalk of your skirt,
roses are not more ruthless than your silver-pink lipstick.

Let me live always and forever among neighbours like these
who order their year by the dates of the leek competitions,
who care sacrificially for Jack Russell terriers and pigeons,
who read very carefully captions in *The Advertiser* and *Echo*
which record their successes and successes of teams they support,
whose daughters grow up and marry friends' boys from Crook.
O wedding gifts, o porcelain flowers
twined on their vases under the lacelip curtains,
save me from Habitat and snobbery and too damn much literary
ambition!

Anne Stevenson

The Butchers

When he had made sure there were no survivors in his house
And that all the suitors were dead, heaped in blood and dust
Like fish that fishermen with fine-meshed nets have hauled
Up gasping for salt water, evaporating in the sunshine,
Odysseus, spattered with muck and like a lion dripping blood
From his chest and cheeks after devouring a farmer's bullock,
Ordered the disloyal housemaids to sponge down the armchairs
And tables, while Telemachos, the oxherd and the swineherd
Scraped the floor with shovels, and then between the portico
And the roundhouse stretched a hawser and hanged the women
So none touched the ground with her toes, like long-winged thrushes
Or doves trapped in a mist-net across the thicket where they roost,
Their heads bobbing in a row, their feet twitching but not for long,
And when they had dragged Melanthios's corpse into the haggard
And cut off his nose and ears and cock and balls, a dog's dinner,
Odysseus, seeing the need for whitewash and disinfectant,
Fumigated the house and the outhouses, so that Hermes
Like a clergyman might wave the supernatural baton
With which he resurrects or hypnotises those he chooses,
And waken and round up the suitors' souls, and the housemaids',
Like bats gibbering in the nooks of their mysterious cave
When out of the clusters that dangle from the rocky ceiling
One of them drops and squeaks, so their souls were bat-squeaks
As they flittered after Hermes, their deliverer, who led them
Along the clammy sheughs, then past the oceanic streams
And the white rock, the sun's gatepost in that dreamy region,
Until they came to a bog-meadow full of bog-asphodels
Where the residents are ghosts or images of the dead.

Michael Longley

On the Beach at Thorpeness

I looked idly right for corpses in the underbrush,
then left, to check that Sizewell was still there.
The wind was from that quarter, northeasterly, a seawind,
B-wind, from that triune reliable fissile block.

– It blackened the drainage ditches
on the low coastal plain, blew up a dry tushing rustle
from the liberal-democratic Aesopian bullrushes,
and an ill-tempered creaking from Christian oaks...

A set of three-point lion prints padded up the beach.
The tideline was a ravel of seaweed and detritus,
a red ragged square of John Bull plastic,
a gull's feather lying down by a fishspine.

The North Sea was a yeasty, sudsy brown slop.
My feet jingled on the sloping gravel,
a crisp musical shingle. My tracks were oval holes
like whole notes or snowshoes or Dover soles.

Roaring waves of fighters headed back to Bentwaters.
The tide advanced in blunt codshead curves,
ebbed through the chattering teeth of the pebbles.
Jaw jaw. War war.

Michael Hofmann

Neighbours

That spring was late. We watched the sky
and studied charts for shouldering isobars.
Birds were late to pair. Crows drank from the lamb's eye.

Over Finland small birds fell: song-thrushes
steering north, smudged signatures on light,
migrating warblers, nightingales.

Wing-beats failed over fjords, each lung a sip of gall.
Children were warned of their dangerous beauty.
Milk was spilt in Poland. Each quarrel

the blowback from some old story,
a mouthful of bitter air from the Ukraine
brought by the wind out of its box of sorrows.

This spring a lamb sips caesium on a Welsh hill.
A child, lifting her face to drink the rain,
takes into her blood the poisoned arrow.

Now we are all neighbourly, each little town
in Europe twinned to Chernobyl, each heart
with the burnt fireman, the child on the Moscow train.

In the democracy of the virus and the toxin
we wait. We watch for bird migrations,
one bird returning with green in its voice,

glasnost,
golau glas,
a first break of blue.

Gillian Clarke

golau glas blue light

The First Men on Mercury

– We come in peace from the third planet.
Would you take us to your leader?

– Bawr stretter! Bawr. Bawr. Stretterhawl?

– This is a little plastic model
of the solar system, with working parts.
You are here and we are there and we
are now here with you, is this clear?

– Gawl horrop. Bawr. Abawrhannahanna!

– Where we come from is blue and white
with brown, you see we call the brown
here 'land', the blue is 'sea', and the white
is 'clouds' over land and sea, we live
on the surface of the brown land,
all round is sea and clouds. We are 'men'.
Men come –

– Glawp men! Gawrbenner menko. Menhawl?

– Men come in peace from the third planet
which we call 'earth'. We are earthmen.
Take us earthmen to your leader.

– Thmen? Thmen? Bawr. Bawrhossop.
Yuleeda tan hanna. Harrabost yuleeda.

– I am the yuleeda. You see my hands,
we carry no benner, we come in peace.
The spaceways are all stretterhawn.

– Glawn peacemen all horrabhanna tantko!
Tan come at' mstrossop. Glawp yuleeda!

– Atoms are peacegawl in our harraban.
Menbat worrabost from tan hannahanna.

– You men we know bawrhossoptant. Bawr.
We know yuleeda. Go strawg backspetter quick.

– We cantantabawr, tantingko backspetter now!

– Banghapper now! Yes, third planet back.
Yuleeda will go back blue, white, brown
nowhanna! There is no more talk.

– Gawl han fasthapper?

No. You must go back to your planet.
Go back in peace, take what you have gained
but quickly.

– Stretterworra gawl, gawl...

– Of course, but nothing is ever the same,
now is it? You'll remember Mercury.

Edwin Morgan

The Second

Aldeburgh Poetry Festival

9 – 11 November 1990

A Sense of History

Judi Benson
David Dabydeen
Carol Ann Duffy
Judy Gahagan
Mick Gowar
Andrew Greig
Miroslav Holub
Herbert Lomas
John Lucas
Gerda Mayer
John Montague
Marin Sorescu
Stephen Spender
Martin Stannard
George Szirtes
Charles Tomlinson
C. K. Williams

Scary Monsters

I love blood
I love gore
Horror movies — give me MORE.

I think Dracula's brilliant
And Frankenstein is a ball,
'Halloween 3'
Is my cup of tea,
'I Spit on your Chainsaw'
I'd queue in the rain for,
'The Unquiet Grave'
Is just what I crave
        And I never get frightened at all.
        No, I never get frightened at all.

I love blood
I love gore
Horror movies — give me MORE.

I adore all the bloodiest moments
Like the scenes when the heads start to fall,
My recreation
Is decapitation,
My lips begin smackin'
When vampires start snackin',
What gets me besotted's
The dripping carotids
        And I never get frightened at all.
        No, I never got frightened at all.

I love blood
I love gore
Horror movies — give me MORE.

But. . . Late at night
When my room is black
And the Zombies prowl
With the Werewolf pack
And the Vampire dares
To climb the stairs

In the wee small hours of the night...

Then Mum stands guard on the landing
And Dad's at the foot of the stairs
While I sit on the loo with the radio on
And the door wide open
And sing my song:

(oh, i love blood,
yes, i love gore,
horror movies – give me more.)

Mick Gowar

All Legendary Obstacles

All legendary obstacles lay between
Us, the long imaginary plain,
The monstrous nick of mountains
And, swinging across the night,
Flooding the Sacramento, San Joaquin,
The hissing drift of winter rain.

All day I waited, shifting
Nervously from station to bar
As I saw another train sail
By, the *San Francisco Chief* or
Golden Gate, water dripping
From great flanged wheels.

At midnight you came, pale
Above the negro porter's lamp.
I was too blind with rain
And doubt to speak, but
Reached from the platform
Until our chilled hands met.

You had been travelling for days
With an old lady, who marked
A neat circle on the glass
With her glove, to watch us
Move into the wet darkness
Kissing, still unable to speak.

John Montague

Make Believe

Say I were not sixty,
say you weren't near-hundred,
say you were alive.
Say my verse was read
in some distant country,
and say you were idly turning the pages:

The blood washed from your shirt,
the tears from your eyes,
the earth from your bones;
neither missing since 1940,
nor dead as reported later
by a friend of a friend of a friend ...

Quite dapper you stand in that bookshop
and chance upon my clues.

That is why at sixty
when some publisher asks me
for biographical details,
I still carefully give
the year of my birth,
the name of my hometown:

GERDA MAYER born '27, in Karlsbad,
Czechoslovakia... write to me, father.

Gerda Mayer

NOTE: The author's father, Arnold Stein, escaped from the German concentration camp in Nisko in 1939, fled to Russian-occupied Lemberg/Lwow, and then disappeared in the summer of 1940. It is thought he may have died in a Russian camp.

Dolphins

Happy, they leap
Out of the surface
Of waves reflecting
The sun fragmented
To broken glass
By the stiff breeze
Across our bows.

Curving, they draw
Curlicues
And serifs with
Lashed tail and fin
Across the screen
Of blue horizon -
Images
Of their delight
Outside, displaying
My heart within.

Across this dazzling
Mediterranean
August morning
The dolphins write such
Ideograms:
With power to wake
Me prisoned in
My human speech
They sign:
'I AM!'

Stephen Spender

Catching Crabs

Ruby and me stalking savannah
Crab season with cutlass and sack like big folk.
Hiding behind stones or clumps of bush
Crabs locked knee-deep in mud mating
And Ruby seven years old feeling strange at the sex
And me horrified to pick them up
Plunge them into the darkness of bag,
So all day we scout to catch the lonesome ones
Who don't mind cooking because they got no prospect
Of family, and squelching through the mud,
Cutlass clearing bush at our feet,
We come home tired slow, weighed down with plenty
Which Ma throw live into boiling pot piece-piece.
Tonight we'll have one big happy curry feed,
We'll test out who teeth and jaw strongest
Who will grow up to be the biggest
Or who will make most terrible cannibal.

We leave behind a mess of bones and shell
And come to England and America
Where Ruby hustles in a New York tenement
And me writing poetry at Cambridge,
Death long catch Ma, the house boarded up
Breeding wasps, woodlice in its dark-sack belly:
I am afraid to walk through weed yard,
Reach the door, prise open, look,
In case the pot still bubbles magical
On the fireside, and I see Ma
Working a ladle, slow-
Limbed, crustacean-old, alone,
In case the woodsmoke and curry steam
Burn my child-eye and make it cry.

David Dabydeen

TRANSLATING THE ENGLISH, 1989

'...and much of the poetry, alas, is lost in translation...'

Welcome to my country! We have here Edwina Currie
and The Sun newspaper. Much excitement.
Also the weather has been most improving
even in February. Daffodils. (Wordsworth. Up North.) If you like
Shakespeare or even Opera we have too the Black Market.
For two hundred quids we are talking Les Miserables,
nods being as good as winks. Don't eat the eggs.
Wheel-clamp. Dogs. Vagrants. A tour of our wonderful
capital city is not to be missed. The Fergie,
The Princess Di and the football hooligan, truly you will
like it here, Squire. Also we can be talking crack, smack
and Carling Black Label if we are so inclined. Don't
drink the H_2O. All very proud we now have
a green Prime Minister. What colour yours? Binbags.
You will be knowing of Charles Dickens and Terry Wogan
and Scotland. All this can be arranged for cash no questions.
Ireland not on. Fish and chips and the Official Secrets Act
second to none. Here we go. We are liking
a smashing good time like estate agents and Neighbours,
also Brookside for we are allowed four Channels.
How many you have? Last night of Proms. Andrew
Lloyd-Webber. Jeffrey Archer. Plenty culture you will be agreeing.
Also history and buildings. The Houses of Lords. Docklands.
Many thrills and high interest rates for own good. Muggers.
Much lead in petrol. Filth. Rule Britannia and child abuse.
Electronic tagging, Boss, ten pints and plenty rape. Queen Mum.
Channel Tunnel. You get here fast no problem to my country
my country my country welcome welcome welcome.

Carol Ann Duffy

Sea Lady

Someone's crept out of the sea,
lying on the pebbles, in pain:
a crippled labrador.
She raises one arm, a lady
in a siesta, languidly,
though night's falling, and this January rain.

Hearing my crunch on the shingle,
she's turning bitch-soft eyes and whiskers to vet me.
I'm coming too close,
and she growls, hisses and whispers,
tensing my tail with her speech,
though I know she can't get me.

Hurt? Perhaps she's tired?
But I'm too close, so she levers her spine
and flops down a shingle bank, enters the ocean,
periscopes twice with her head,
then hoists ashore,
crutching her legless rear up the steep incline.

Who'd be sick, if they lived in the ocean?
And who'd bark
so hard after fish, they'd give up the earth,
lose hands and legs,
freezing the warm blood back
to the cold, to feel after fish in the dark?

I sit in my lights by the fire, listening to Mozart,
reading Gibbon.
A Diocletian legionary, an old lag
looking for loot, found
a beautiful leather purse of priceless pearls.
He threw the swag away and kept the bag.

For what's no use can have no value.
And in the morning she
who loves the waters I left behind
is gone like a piece of flotsam,
a bag of pearls,
that is and always will be far out at sea.

Herbert Lomas

Says The Southerner

Hot? Why you don't know the half of it.
Wait til your steerin wheel melts on down
to soft plastic so's you can't even turn it
and the backs of your legs get 3rd degree
burns from the seat and a waverin line
hovers just above street level over hot tar

and creosote. Wait till the deepest water
turns to soup weighs you down,
contradicting buoyancy and you opens your mouth
for a gulp of air and nothin happens
cause it ain't movin and not your limbs either.
And your brain can't find its tongue,

one syllable turns to three and you can't even
raise your hand to swat some fly
that's kinda slow motion on your face
or else it died, like right there.
Your stomach kinda does its own heave lurch
one-two like it wants to turn inside out

'cept there's not enough liquid
to get a good retch goin and you can't tell
the difference anyhow from the shower
and your own sweat and every sound is intensified.
Wait til your passion stops being some sex hump
touch me touch me o yeah baby right there...

But instead you thinks you gonna go crazy
if he don't just take his hot body over there
somewhere out of reach. 'Sides he's suckin
up all your oxygen. And you become cicada
only wantin it every seventeen years
or leastwise only in winter. Now that's hot.

Judi Benson

Mourning

At first, the landscape of your face
shone clear as the full moon's seas,
filling my eyelid's window, fitting perfectly.

Sometimes I would take you like a watch from my pocket
and examine your features secretly,
counting them.

You gazed back willingly, just as I had left you,
and even spoke words I had chosen for you.

Then I held your plaster head between my hands
and, like a god with puffed cheeks,
blew life onto your brow.

I put you close to my ear to hear your breath
and heard only my own. I looked again.
Your eye-sockets were empty, your mask
indifferent, your lips
a dead emperor's.

My fingers crumbled you to the finest powder
that would fit a funeral urn
the size of a matchbox.

Judy Gahagan

Phil's Poem

I've decided to be nice to everyone
and not tell any more lies;
but with the sun shining on this brilliant
November evening I have to go into some family history
before things can even begin to come clear –
Stannards have never been possessed of the pioneer spirit,
they have never stood at the edge of the prairie
and seen a little chunk of it in their mind's eye
and wanted to make it their own,
they have never saluted the star-spangled banner,
and they have never been called Phil. What's more,
Stannards have never been famous, they have never
stood out in a crowd, they have never been mentioned
in dispatches, they have never contributed much
to debates, charities, culture or suggestion boxes,
they have never been rich, they have never
been slung in jail, they have never lusted openly
but kept it to themselves (like smoke), they have
never learnt to swim, not even when their heads
were being held under water, they have never marched,
struck, protested, demonstrated or complained,
they have never spoken what was on their minds
because they have never had much on their minds
worth speaking of, they have never cared much
for style, or suffering if that suffering was
more than an arm's length distant, and they have never
been missed after they were gone, because
they have never been noticed while they were there.
Some things can, perhaps, now become clear.

Martin Stannard

Studying Grosz On The Bus

His prick of a cigar
hanging from pouchy lips,
her marcelled mouth ajar,
the avid way she sips
schnapps – is it? – or crème-
de-menthe, above torn stocking
a spread of mottled thigh.
Eyes like leaky phlegm
swim in their faces, shocking
Grosz to a sour disgust
and definition, so *die*
liebe translates to *lust.*

And this pair on the bus,
they've come straight from his art:
him all corm nose, her
raddled, ridiculous
face, her mangy fur;
and look at how they cart
bulging bags of shop
stuff, bought for a week
's swill and snout!
                                        But it stops
short, this willed hate. They speak,
you see, and I've heard
each scuffed, penny-plain word
passing from man to wife,
the small change of a life
that rings clear to the heart
of the matter: life's other than art.

John Lucas

A Picture of My Parents with their First Television

I see them before the television, the proud owners
of a wooden case in which the four-o-five
presents its milky versions of success
with the last official faces of a time
that was always more dead than alive,
when Hanratty cleaned the windows and a crime
was solved by men with briefcases and bowlers,
when gentlemen made jokes in evening dress.

They fought their way to this, to Lady Barnett
to Bernard Braden and John Freeman, Kathie Kay
and Alan Breeze, to all those names of power
that solved nothing but could somehow fill
the hours before they slipped away
to private lives which grew more private still,
past old reliable faces by which they set
their clocks precisely to the latest hour.

Some blurred depth in their eyes won't come to rest:
perhaps they're trapped in what they bought,
in all their trappings, in the slim white frame
of the square photograph they sent back home
to show the television. Now they're caught
and solemn. Slowly they become
the stillness by which they are both possessed.
They're listening intently for a name

which once had power, on lips that formed the sound
in darkened flats, in beds in which they slept
and touched each other. Some act of violence
has pitched them here before the screen.
The actors know their speeches, are adept
at pulling faces, know when to go. They've been
elsewhere and are there still, on neutral ground,
of which this patch of grey is evidence.

George Szirtes

The Fox Gallery

A long house –
the fox gallery you called
its upper storey, because
you could look down to see
(and did) the way a fox would
cross the field beyond
and you could follow out, window
to window, the fox's way
the whole length of the meadow
parallel with the restraining line
of wall and pane, or as far
as that could follow the sense of all
those windings. Do you remember
the morning I woke you with the cry
Fox fox and the animal
came on – not from side
to side, but straight
at the house and we craned
to see more and more, the most
we could of it and then
watched it sheer off deterred
by habitation, and saw
how utterly the two worlds were
disparate, as that perfect
ideogram for agility
and liquefaction flowed
away from us rhythmical
and flickering and
that flare was final.

Charles Tomlinson

from: A Flame in Your Heart

'Finest summer I remember' Old George says
without irony, straightening his hollyhocks.
Right enough, the sun day after day
and nowhere to hide in the sky, men charred
to wavering black sticks against the glare,
then soft thuds in the night, fruit-fall
and bruised lovers giggling in the lanes...

Wasps crawled from the plums she picked
but were too groggy to fly or sting
and I felt drugged with heavy juice,
leaning to flick them from her arm...

'Keep out of mischief' Old George leers
and hee-haws as he shuffles off, leaving me
fingers clenched round a windfall Cox's
still fizzling at the edge of my last bite –
I sling it away and hurry to find her
before heat goes out of the day.

Andrew Greig

Omens

If you meet a chair,
that is good, you will go to Heaven.
If you meet a mountain,
that is bad, you'll go to the chair.
If you meet the Great Bear,
that is good, you will go to Heaven.
If you meet a snail,
that is bad, you'll go to the snail.
If you meet a woman,
that is good, you will go to Heaven.
If you meet a tablecloth,
that is bad, you'll go to the cupboard.
If you meet a snake,
that is good, it will die and you'll go to Heaven.
If the snake meets you,
that is bad, you will die and the snake go to Heaven.

If you die,
that's bad, bad.

Beware of this omen
and of all others.

Marin Sorescu

My Mother's Lips

Until I asked her to please stop doing it and was astonished to find that
she not only could
but from the moment I asked her in fact would stop doing it, my mother,
all through my childhood,
when I was saying something to her, something important, would move
her lips as I was speaking
so that she seemed to be saying under her breath the very words I was
saying as I was saying them.

Or, even more disconcertingly – wildly so now that my puberty had
erupted – *before* I said them.
When I was smaller, I must just have assumed that she was omniscient.
Why not?
She knew everything else – when I was tired, or lying; she'd know I was
ill before I did.
I may even have thought – how could it not have come into my mind?
– that she *caused* what I said.

All she was really doing of course was mouthing my words a split second
after I said them myself,
but it wasn't until my own children were learning to talk that I really
understood how,
and understood, too, the edge of anxiety in it, the wanting to bring you
along out of the silence,
the compulsion to lift you again from those blank caverns of nameless-
ness we encase.

That was long afterward, though: where I was now was just wanting
to get her to stop,
and, considering how I brooded and raged in those days, how quickly
my teeth went on edge,
the restraint I approached her with seems remarkable, although her so
unprotestingly,
readily taming a habit by then three children and a dozen years old was
as much so.

It's endearing to watch us again in that long-ago dusk, facing each other,
my mother and me.
I've just grown to her height, or just past it: there are our lips moving
together,
now the unison suddenly breaks, I have to go on by myself, no maestro,
no score to follow.
I wonder what finally made me take umbrage enough, or heart enough,
to confront her?

It's not important. My cocoon at that age was already unwinding: the
threads ravel and snarl.
When I find one again, it's that two o'clock in the morning, a grim hotel
on a square,
the impenetrable maze of an endless city, when, really alone for the first
time in my life,
I found myself leaning from the window, incanting in a tearing whisper
what I thought were poems.

I'd love to know what I raved that night to the night, what those innocent
dithyrambs were,
or to feel what so ecstatically drew me out of myself and beyond . . .
Nothing is there, though,
only the solemn piazza beneath me, the riot of dim, tiled roofs and
impassable alleys,
my desolate bed behind me, and my voice, hoarse, and the sweet, alien
air against me like a kiss.

C. K. Williams

Brief Reflection on Cats Growing in Trees

When moles still had their annual general meetings
  and when they still had better eyesight it befell
  that they expressed a wish to discover what
  was above.
So they elected a commission to ascertain what was above.
The commission despatched a sharp-sighted fleet-footed
  mole. He, having left his native mother earth,
  caught sight of a tree with a bird on it.

Thus a theory was put forward that up above
  birds grew on trees. However,
  some moles thought this was
  too simple. So they despatched another
  mole to ascertain if birds did grow on trees.

By then it was evening and on the tree
  some cats were mewing. Mewing cats,
  the second mole announced, grew on the tree.
Thus an alternative theory emerged about cats.

The two conflicting theories bothered an elderly
  neurotic member of the commission. And he
  climbed up to see for himself.
By then it was night and all was pitch-black.

Both schools are mistaken, the venerable mole declared.
  Birds and cats are optical illusions produced
  by the refraction of light. In fact, things above

Were the same as below, only the clay was less dense and
  the upper roots of the trees were whispering something,
  but only a little.

And that was that.

Ever since the moles have remained below ground:
  they do not set up commissions
  or presuppose the existence of cats.

Or if so only a little.

Miroslav Holub

The Third

Aldeburgh Poetry Festival

8 – 10 November 1991

Ends & Beginnings

Donald Atkinson
Patricia Beer
James Berry
Alan Brownjohn
Liz Cashdan
Nina Cassian
Charles Causley
Tony Curtis
Adam Czerniawski
Janet Fisher
Michael Hulse
Jackie Kay
Kenneth Koch
Christine McNeill
Anne Rouse
Carol Rumens
Joan Jobe Smith
Fred Voss
Kit Wright

Wailing Begins at the House-wall

Wailing begins at the house-wall where as a child
I would rust lips kissing the rough brick dado,
rub my forehead on it till it bled, then
falling to bruised knees drag down brailled fingers' ends
through a crumble of mortar till my mother called:
stop eating the house, it's dirty!
Adding an anal phoneme – a'a (caca, shit.)

Indoors she feeds the mangle endless lasagne of washing,
worries because I'm rising three and haven't talked,
busy myself instead with dumb flowers, or seek
identity through injuries. In the sagging
romper-suit she's knitted me (there was a photograph)
I climb the bandy pylon legs of the cast-iron mangle,
feel out its leprosy of blistered green paint.
My mother on the blind side plunges away with the wheel.
When my fingers minced in the cogs' teeth, the pain
froze in my throat and she went on turning
till I fell to the floor with blood enough to
soak the towel she wrapped my shredded hand in.
Our doctor pudged it back to shape and wondered at my
dumbness.
But I had more than that to shut my mouth on then.

A sister came. We bathe her, my mother and I,
in the rough zinc tub by the fire. First
sample the water with lemon elbows, then gently
immerse our ecstatic pink dough. When we soap her tum
her limbs weave little epilepsies with the air,
her buttocks cradled in the hand are like a stiff hot jelly.
My mother lets me fingertip the pulse
where the bones of the skull haven't closed yet.
For a moment I touch the soft spillable life so thinly sealed.
Who would not want to be her mother? I did.
Or with her in those waters still.

Were we breast-fed? I can't remember it. Only how
from the first dither of an eyelash, Dad, you
hung over us like an axe. Smacked us to sleep.
They say my sister died in your vigils. Six months
breathed under your hand, skin-crazed with eczema.
Each night you turned her onto her sore side,
and when she cried at that you slapped her face.
This was our Margaret and you unleaved her.

Donald Atkinson

from: THE ADOPTION PAPERS

The first agency we went to
didn't want us on their lists,
we didn't live close enough to a church
nor were we church-goers
(though we kept quiet about being communists).
The second told us
we weren't high enough earners.
The third liked us
but they had a five-year waiting list.
I spent six months trying not to look
at swings nor the front of supermarket trolleys,
not to think this kid I've wanted could be five.
The fourth agency was full up.
The fifth said yes but again no babies.
Just as we were going out the door
I said oh you know we don't mind the colour.
Just like that, the waiting was over.

Jackie Kay

The Automatic Days

And they finally arrived at the grey pit
Between the Xmas rush and the New Year Sales;
Which you could fall into and not be thought of,
And lie there gazing up at a paper bell
Tangled round with bows of artificial silk,
Looking frayed and stained in the draught from the swing doors,
While the days did not draw in and would not draw out,
And the sunsets came cold and frail. Going through
PINE MIRRORS: HUGE REDUCTIONS, Beverley's face
Is reduced to a summary of the months
Since spring; she shakes her hair across its learnt
Grimaces, will she stop for the New Year?

Next day she stops at a particular
Pine Mirror, a line rather hard to sell,
And fixes in it a special rigid stare.
Far away behind her in slow miniature,
She sees Mrs Gurnard and Tamsin listening
While Trevor tells a joke, automatic days
Are passing while she stands there. Everyone
Knows of the moment when you choose between
Yourself and the mirror they give you. Beverley,
Seeing all of Goodbody's waiting for her to move,
Pushes her hair back and controls her lips;
Braces her spirit and walks right on through.

Alan Brownjohn

Roadworkers Picking Cherries

The first, wearing rumpled cords belted with clothes-line,
  climbs on the wall where the shade crumples and
flaps, and takes off the hat that reminds him of the
  wine he drank sitting under a fig tree
in a Sicilian village. The straw is frayed
  and feathering at the crown, but he holds
the hat in a pinch of affection, the fonder
  of it the more it weathers, and fans the
air to cool his face. From the fields the laughter of
  children. The fragrance of hay. He reaches
up to the dark blood-coloured cherries and plucks and
  drops a fruit in his hat, then another,
and goes on picking, contented, feeling the warmth
  of the afternoon. It is good. His hat
is filling.
          The younger man in blue overalls
  is thinking how peaceful the silence is
now they've switched off the generator.
                                        Soon there are
  five of them up on the wall, picking and
laughing and spitting the stones in the orchard grass,
  and the man with the hat has eaten through
to the base of the crown, which is stained with juice, and
  he sits at the dusty roadside, and pulls
the brim of his hat to shadow his brow, hearing
  the single excitement of a lark and
knowing the dark red stains in his hat will forever
  recall a day when he sat with the taste
of cherries in his mouth and looked out on the fields
  fading to pale blue in the distant hills.

Michael Hulse

SOUP

One night our block leader set a competition:
two bowls of soup to the best teller of a tale.
That whole evening the hut filled with words –
tales from the old countries
of wolves and children
potions and love-sick herders
stupid woodsmen and crafty villagers.
Apple-blossom snowed from blue skies,
orphans discovered themselves royal.
Tales of greed and heroes and cunning survival,
soldiers of the Empires, the Church, the Reich.

And when they turned to me
I could not speak,
sunk in the horror of that place,
my throat a corridor of bones, my eyes
and nostrils clogged with self-pity.
'Speak,' they said, 'everyone has a story to tell.'
And so I closed my eyes and said:
I have no hunger for your bowls of soup, you see
I have just risen from the Shabbat meal –
my father has filled our glasses with wine,
bread has been broken, the maid has served fish.
Grandfather has sung, tears in his eyes, the old songs.
My mother holds her glass by the stem, lifts
it to her mouth, the red glow reflecting on her throat.
I go to her side and she kisses me for bed.
My grandfather's kiss is rough and soft like an apricot.
The sheets on my bed are crisp and flat
like the leaves of a book...

I carried my prizes back to my bunk: one bowl
I hid, the other I stirred
and smelt a long time, so long
that it filled the cauldron of my head,
drowning a family of memories.

Tony Curtis

From Lucy: A Favour

Leela, darlin', as we did talk,
go an' see the piece of lan'
Cousin Man-Man buy for me. I glad
it near the sea an' not mount'n
lan'. It planted well I hear.
Coconuts, bananas, sugar cane
an' some food growin'. A good
house spot is there, what I will
get raised up little by little.

I more peaceful I get that lan'.
Money here is too dry: can't
turn it in a pig or goat, only
comforts, what make me ashame
sometimes. Ashame too how
neighbours supply dustbins
with loaves, with half chickens,
with good clothes.

Nowadays I don't eat in a day
or two, I sing to meself. I think
of air we breathe, water
we drink an' sun that shine.
I don't let the man touch
me V-centre place.

Darlin', a parcel on the way
for you. Go an' see the piece
of lan' for me. Soon I'll come
again an' walk on it
in breeze what touch the sun
an' swing coconut limbs.

Walk good, Leela, chile.
'Walk-good keeps good spirit.'

James Berry

Cutting Loose

Cut-outs today, her mother said,
Showing her how to manoeuvre finger and thumb.
She remembers those nursery days
Blunt-ended scissors refusing to turn
Neat corners, leaving white half moons
Like unexpected halos.
Sometimes the wilful blades would chop off limbs,
Slit faces in their clumsy surgery.

Now as she sorts and cuts the photographs
Her bungling anger leaves his severed arm
Still guiding hers towards their wedding cake.
And when she has to face the family groups
He's so hemmed in, the others suffer
Lacerations she only meant for him.

Liz Cashdan

Fifty Years On

it's Quiz Night at the Chamberlain Arms and Frank
has written the questions himself this time.
Jane, Irma and I, drinking ginger wine, drying up
on England captains and the length of snooker tables,

squeeze fragments of gossip into the gaps.
The Vicar has been asked to bless the Scout
Hut as a rates dodge, it's part of the job
like praying for the dead and always smiling,

but Jane comparing the Cubs to Hitler Youth is probably
tactless: Irma's father was in the Luftwaffe,
a P.O.W. who stayed on. Irma hates Poles
and Communists. We're into the second half and Frank

is hotting up the humour. Which United player is
a German newspaper? Zy Tung? Dee Velt? The answer
is Gerry Daley, Jane declares it's racist and Irma
pinks up. Later over coffee she pounces on my

Tradescantia. Do let me have a piece of your
Wandering Jew, she exclaims, waving the scissors.

Janet Fisher

Geography Lesson

He looked out the window when he asked
the capital of Uruguay,
the largest river in China.

He asked us the main agricultural
product of Albania
and still looked out the window.

An aircraft circled in a precise sky.
'Buenos Aires,' Karl said.
'Wrong,' he replied. 'Montevideo.'

We made another effort: 'Yellow River.'
'Can't wait to get away, can you?'
We smirked — *he* could talk.

In his eyes shifted ochre (for the unadventurous),
turquoise for the girls,
aquamarine for the deep ones.

Legs a single bone
he turned and muttered: 'Theresienstadt,
Auschwitz, Mauthausen.'

Then took the rubber,
erased his drawing of Germany
on the blackboard.

We thought him nuts,
a casualty of years of sameness.
But the names clung.

Vietnam. Israel. Nicaragua.
He is dead now, we think.
And watch through our windows.

Christine McNeill

Sacrificial Wolf

The careful suburban dead turn their backs
On this squat of sodden grass,
Hedged by the Finchley traffic:
The vicar poised like a prowhead
Over the shameless pit, answered
By a hectoring gull. It brings back
The afternoons in the dry houses,
The hostels and clinic waiting-rooms,
When you with the cor anglais of a shout
Parted the smokers' fug,
Flattering social workers with quotes
From Wilde or Krishnamurti –
Such was the splendour and disgrace
That only a few of us have come to light
Our makeshift Roman candles, bitten shy:
An elegy, my friend, dear wolf,
Being just your sort of con.

Anne Rouse

from: A Meeting of Innocents: A Birthday Sequence

6

It was the crying hand
Thrust from the shawl, unannounced
As celandines in cold March grass.

It was the five little swimmers,
Waxed in each wrinkle and seam,
Bent at the waist, sea-wearied.

It was the stronghold they shut
Round her probing finger, the way
The crying shivered into stillness,

That made her think that the teeming
Shambles of it all was planned,
And the plan was matchless.

Carol Rumens

In a Country Museum

This is a strange museum. In one square yard see
A mummified ibis and a postilion's boot.
Grey litter fills the house. For years every dead man
Had some cast-off curious object to donate.

Mindless and slovenly it is, but in one room,
Close to five jars that once held Daffy's Elixir,
Lies something that takes shape. A pallid patchwork quilt
Wrapped in cellophane, is spread on a four-poster.

A card describes the maker, a fourteen-year-old
Servant girl, with no book-learning and no siblings,
Who saved up half-a-crown for the big central piece
Of cloth, and got up at dawn on summer mornings.

This sounds sober and worthy, but the card goes on
To say that, interviewed at eighty, Mrs Brew
Declared it had given her much greater pleasure
Than anything in all her life. If it is true

That to labour on these plodding squares meant more
Than marriage bed, children and a belief in God,
It is the best country marvel in this building
And suitably placed among these bright fields of food.

Patricia Beer

Eden Rock

They are waiting for me somewhere beyond Eden Rock:
My father, twenty-five, in the same suit
Of Genuine Irish Tweed, his terrier Jack
Still two years old and trembling at his feet.

My mother, twenty-three, in a sprigged dress
Drawn at the waist, ribbon in her straw hat,
Has spread the stiff white cloth over the grass.
Her hair, the colour of wheat, takes on the light.

She pours tea from a Thermos, the milk straight
From an old H.P. sauce-bottle, a screw
Of paper for a cork; slowly sets out
The same three plates, the tin cups painted blue.

The sky whitens as if lit by three suns.
My mother shades her eyes and looks my way
Over the drifted stream. My father spins
A stone along the water. Leisurely,

They beckon to me from the other bank.
I hear them call, 'See where the stream-path is!
Crossing is not as hard as you might think.'

I had not thought that it would be like this.

Charles Causley

Underneath the Archers
or
What's all this about Walter's Willy?

Everyone's on about Walter's willy
  Down at the Bull tonight.
He's done Dan's sheep and he's done them silly –
He's had young Phil and his daughter's filly –
  And folk don't think it's right.

  Folk *know* it can't be right.

No, the chat's not prim and the chat's not proper,
  Down at the Bull tonight,
'Cos everyone's on about Walter's whopper
And telling tales of his terrible chopper –
  And folk don't think it's right.

Sid Perks has drained the bitter cup
  Down at the Bull tonight.
Can't stand. . . or sit. . . or speak. . . or sup. . .
Walter got him while bottling up –
  And folk don't think it's right.

  Folk *know* it can't be right.

He got poor Polly while drawing a cork
  Down at the Bull tonight.
And Doris is still too ill to talk –
And Mrs Perkins can hardly walk –
  And folk don't think it's right.

There's in-depth discussion of every facet,
  Down at the Bull tonight,
Of Walter's gigantic natural asset –
Carries as far as Penny Hasset –
  (Folk know that can't be right)

  Folk *know* it can't be right.

Poor old Dan's a broken man
  Down at the Bull tonight.
Got locked in the back of Walter's van
With its ghastly height, unearthly span –
  And folk don't think it's right.

Found him alone in the woods on Sunday
  (Down at the Bull tonight),
Had him all day and most of Monday –
That was the end of poor Joe Grundy –
  Folk don't think it's right.

  Folk *know* it can't be right.

It wasn't a Gainsborough nor an El Greco
  (Down at the Bull tonight)
Brought dozens of coach-loads out for a dekko –
But a photo-fit in the *Borchester Echo* –
  Folk don't think it's right.

Nobody understands it fully,
  Down at the Bull tonight,
The monstrous *range* of it. Was it by pulley
It scaled Grey Gables and whopped Jack Woolley?
  Folk don't think it's right.

  Folk *know* it can't be right.

There's coaches come from Ware and Wigan,
  Down at the Bull tonight,
From Wales and Wallasey, out for a swig an'
A sizing-up of Walter's big 'un –
  And folk don't think it's right.

Yes, everyone's on about Walter's thuggery,
  Down at the Bull tonight,
His *cattle*-courting, his *sheep* skullduggery,
Piggery jiggery-pokery buggery –
  Folk don't think it's right.

  Folk *know* it can't be right.

Even the Vicar's been muttering, 'F* * * it,'
  Down at the Bull tonight,
'There's nowhere left he hasn't stuck it –
I *wish* old Walter would kick the bucket –
  He knows it can't be right!'

  Folk know it CAN'T BE RIGHT!

Kit Wright

On the Way to Heaven

She nearly died the year before she
really died. I saved her, gave her
mouth-to-mouth, pounded her chest,
like they do in the movies - bruising
her - until she finally came to, and
like in the movies, smiled, looked
around, and asked, 'Where am I?' When I
told her, and that I'd brought her to,
she said, oh, no, you ruined everything,
I was on my way to heaven, heard angels
singing, I was dressed all in white and
had no more pain. She wept all morning.

In the afternoon she called me into her
room and sternly told me that if that
ever happened again, not to save her.
I told her I couldn't help trying to
save her, that something stronger than
me made me do it, a reflex perhaps from
the womb like when she'd yank my hand
in time to save me from being run over by
a car. She screamed at me all afternoon
from her room how I'd ruined it for her,
and would again, and I screamed back how
sick I was of all this: the bedpans, the
morphine, my keeping her alive for her to
wish she'd die. Such ingratitude!
We both wept till dinnertime.

While I fed her dessert of ice cream,
she cleared her throat, letting me
know more was to come, but she apologized
instead, thanked me for saving her life.

‘I know now how much you really must
love me,’ she said, ‘to save this old
bag of worthless bones.’ Then she laughed
for the first time in a long, long time.
I wanted to hug her, but I couldn’t for
her pain. I’d never hug her, I knew,
ever again, but it felt good to both of us
when I cooled her bruises with a little
witch-hazel-soaked cotton swab.

Joan Jobe Smith

Variations on a Theme by William Carlos Williams

1

I chopped down the house that you had been saving to live in
next summer.
I am sorry, but it was morning, and I had nothing to do
and its wooden beams were so inviting.

2

We laughed at the hollyhocks together
and then I sprayed them with lye.
Forgive me. I simply do not know what I am doing.

3

I gave away the money that you had been saving to live on for the
next ten years.
The man who asked for it was shabby
and the firm March wind on the porch was so juicy and cold.

4

Last evening we went dancing and I broke your leg.
Forgive me. I was clumsy, and
I wanted you here in the wards, where I am the doctor!

Kenneth Koch

Fish

he fashioned a poem like a fish
the fish is a symbol of saints
it lives in the depths of secretive seas
and resists massive atmospheric pressures
its presence heralds mysteries
it fell into the nets of mankind
and lies cold on a moist slab
each of its verses has immaculate rhythm
scales of its metaphors glisten in the sun
eyes masked in film live in imagination
and when only the skeleton remains
a white negative of symmetrical pine
words will survive illegibly for ever

Adam Czerniawski

Uptight

Bob tightens the nuts
down onto the clamps.
He is grunting and grimacing,
his biceps straining
and his back nearly wrenching out
as he turns red and tugs on a 2-foot-long crescent wrench,
digging his boot heels into the concrete floor.
He gets out a 4-foot-long section of steel pipe
and slips it over the crescent wrench,
grabbing the pipe as if it were an oar,
leaning back,
giving 4 final tugs
that make the nuts and bolts creak
as if they are about to snap.

The slab of aluminum he must cut is now anchored
to the machine table with more than twice the torque
required to keep extremely hard heat-treated
tool steel
from moving under the force of cutting.

Bob doesn't want that son-of-a-bitch
on night shift
to think that he can tighten nuts
tighter than Bob can.

Fred Voss

Temptation

Call yourself alive? Look, I promise you
that for the first time you'll feel your pores opening
like fish mouths, and you'll actually be able to hear
your blood surging through all those lanes,
and you'll feel light gliding across the cornea
like the train of a dress. For the first time
you'll be aware of gravity
like a thorn in your heel,
and your shoulder blades will ache for want of wings.
Call yourself alive? I promise you
you'll be deafened by dust falling on the furniture,
you'll feel your eyebrows turning to two gashes,
and every memory you have – will begin
at Genesis.

Nina Cassian

The Fourth

Aldeburgh Poetry Festival

13 – 15 November 1992

Thresholds

Moniza Alvi
Connie Bensley
Sujata Bhatt
Duncan Curry
Michael Hamburger
Geoff Hattersley
Jeanette Hattersley
Sylvia Kantaris
Brendan Kennelly
John Latham
Grevel Lindop
Sorley MacLean
Jack Mapanje
John Mole
Sean O'Brien
Bernard O'Donoghue
Mark Roper
Myra Schneider

Alice and Alice

Arm in arm, Alice and Alice
Have walked through the mirror on the wall
And though neither of them is pretty at all
They are both of them nice.

They are going to teach the Queen some manners,
Nobody should behave like that,
And a hatter is no excuse for his hat.
They detest caterpillars.

A race is a race. Someone must win,
And beautiful soup is a matter of taste.
When a cynical cat dissolves with such haste
It should not leave its grin.

This time the sense will take care of the sound,
Language will banish the Jabberwock,
Minutes will do as they're told by the clock
And rabbits will stay underground.

Simply begin as you mean to go on.
If the Queen should cry 'Off with her head!'
Alice and Alice are well enough bred
To know two are better than one.

Croquet is played with mallet and hoops,
Flamingoes aren't held by the leg.
If you're silly enough to try mending an egg
You won't need horses and troops.

The trouble with nonsense is that it's not true
Though the bottle says *Drink me who dares.*
Common sense walks like policemen in pairs
And reason stands to.

So Alice and Alice, arm in arm,
Whom nothing shall ever put asunder,
Have set out to vanquish the forces of wonder.
They mean no harm.

John Mole

Cleaning Ladies

Through the cloisters of the academy
go the round women
brides of the broom
sisters of sweeping
swollen pods of toil

who wait at the pithead
who wait at the docks
who wait by the phone

whose reward is bingo
whose reward is cancer
whose reward is the church

pillars of society
fillers of vacuum
psalters of earth

through the groves of academia
go the swollen girls
moss in their stony wornout wombs
bluebells of smoke in their lungs

who like a bit of sauce
who make ends meet
who go without saying

Mark Roper

A Friendship

He made restless forays
into the edge of our marriage.
One Christmas Eve he came late,
his dark hair crackling with frost,
and ate his carnation buttonhole
to amuse the baby.

When I had a second child
he came to the foot of my bed at dusk
bringing pineapples and champagne,
whispering 'Are you awake?' –
singing a snatch of opera.
The Nurse tapped him on the shoulder.

At the end, we took turns at his bedside.
I curled up in the chair; listened to each breath
postponing itself indefinitely.
He opened his eyes once and I leaned forward:
'Is there anything you want?'
'Now she asks,' he murmured.

Connie Bensley

HMS Glasshouse

At this hour the park offers only
A steam-heated acre of glass,
A sign in fresh hardboard, and somewhere
To wait while appearing to act.

We step inside its vaulted heat,
Its bleared below-decks light. We taste
Its air of rot and counter-rot, attend
Its vegetable politics, and watch

As plants with webbed and shellacked hands
Swarm up the stanchions, offering
The universal shrug of making do,
Like the teenagers painting the catwalks,

Who might once have painted the hulls
Of the frigates and merchantmen sent
To secure the Malvinas for mutton.
Their status as national assets has lapsed

And the registers cancel their names:
They are guilty again, as am I, as are you,
As the glasshouse sweats on
Like the *Unterseeboot* of the state

With its periscope down, its orders sealed,
Its routine a deliberate torpor.
We wake in the very same place
With the curious notion that fish

Have been crowding the glass to peer in
At the items preserved for the voyage –
Cast-iron and Pilkingtons' finest,
Odd volumes of Oakeshott and Scruton

To kill off the time, in an atmosphere
Soon to be poison. Let's make our inspection
On tiptoe, and listen for cracks
In case one of us throws the first stone.

Sean O'Brien

Summer Pudding

for Carole Reeves

Begin with half a pound of raspberries
picked from the deep end of your sloping garden, where the birds
play hopscotch in the draggled fruitnets; add
a quarter of redcurrants; gently seethe in orange juice
for six or seven minutes with some sugar,
giving the pan a ritual shake from time to time, inducing
a marriage of those fine, compatible
tastes; and leave to cool. An open kitchen door invites
whatever breeze will help itself to flavour,
attenuating it downhill across your neighbours' gardens
(be generous!) so summer will surprise them,
an unidentifiable recalled fulfilment haunting
the giant bellflower and the scarlet runners.
Now introduce your strawberries, sliced to let the pallid heartsflesh
transfuse its juice into the mass, transmute
cooled fruit to liquid crystal while you line your bowl with bread
and add the mixture – keeping back some juice –
lid it with bread, cover and weight it, chill it if you like
(as if the winter took a hand) and hoard it,
opus magnum ripening its secret, edible,
inviolable time. And when you dare
slide your knife round its socket to uncling – a sudden suck -
this gelid Silbury mined with the wealth
of archetypal summer, let it be on one of three
occasions: for a kitchenful of children
whose mouths grow purpleringed and flecked with whipped
cream as they dig
and lose, entranced, the treasure of the minute;
or for the friends around your polished table, when that soft
lake of mahogany reflects the faces
melting in candlelight and burgundy, rivers of talk
eddying to a stillness lost in taste
primitive as a language, clear as thought; or for whoever
will join you in your garden when the sun
carries out summer to the edge of dark, and stay to eat
there in the early chill as twilight gels

and owlhoots quiver from the gulf of darkness, where a floodlit
  cathedral floats under your eyes, and still
(wreckage of smeared plates and clotted spoons piling the table)
  after the lights are killed and the cathedral
vanishes like a switchedoff hologram, remain to plot
  the moon's progress across the brimming air
scaled by the nightscented stocks, or with binoculars
  arrest the Brownian movement of the stars.

Grevel Lindop

A Noted Judge of Horses

The ache in his right arm worsening
Morning by morning asks for caution.
He knows its boding, cannot be wrong
About this. Yet he is more concerned
For the planks in the float that need
Woodworm treatment before drawing in
The hay, and whether the coarse meadow
Must be limed before it will crop again.

Still in the pallid dawn he dresses
In the clothes she laid out last night,
Washes in cold water and sets off,
Standing in the trailer with his eyes set
On the Shrove Fair. As long as his arm
Can lift a stick to lay in judgement
Down the shuddering line of a horse's back,
He'll take his chance, ignoring his dream
That before September's fair he'll be mumbling
From a hospital bed, pleading with nurses
To loose the pony tied by the western gate.

Bernard O'Donoghue

An Innocent Adultery

Because love was improper in the flesh
I called him from his house on the dunes
this morning in the early light
when lips rise quietly like fish
and afterwards we lay between two sand hills
on a bed of shells, delicately tinted
with intermingled sea-lights like our skins,
and ground them under our sheer weightlessness
while she stood on the high step of the house
and smiled to see us there
outside the locked door of the granary,
her cheeks as generous as apples,
her basket laden with the good, whole bread
and covered with a cloth for the picnic
on the beach where we three ate
and drank wine like a merry sacrament,
cupping shells most lightly in our hands
as people do when they are innocent.
The whole affair lies quietly on my conscience
although the day before was just the kind
of day for touching breasts, as he had said
casually, as if words had no fingers.

Sylvia Kantaris

Indian Cooking

The bottom of the pan was a palette –
paprika, cayenne, dhania
haldi, heaped like powder-paints.

Melted ghee made lakes, golden rivers.
The keema frying, my mother waited
for the fat to bubble to the surface.

Friends brought silver-leaf.
I dropped it on khir –
special rice pudding for parties.

I tasted the landscape, customs
of my father's country –
its fever on biting a chilli.

Moniza Alvi

The Bottom Back Nut

It's the sort of place you can't get
a half inch drive socket to, a knuckle
joint, a ten mill or a hammer. You can't
get round it because of the sump, you
can't reach it because you're not an orang-u-tan.

The sort where you're trying to
get, cursing at the speck in your
eyeball, when the neighbour says, cheerily
'having trouble?' The sort of place you
laugh off, wiping grease across your

cheek as you do so, where you break your
best screwdriver, smashing your knuckles against the
radiator's rusty back. It's that
place to get to properly, you need two
hundred quid's worth of tackle and

you could drop it off in twenty minutes. As it
is, in the road with a doubtful jack and wet
on your neck and your wife saying 'I'm
off now love', it will take you three
hours and you still won't have done it.

Duncan Curry

Nobel Prize Poem

He awoke with no hangover
because he'd had no beer
and looked in the mirror.
He couldn't help noticing
that a box of old records
not worth listening to
teetered on his neck
in place of a head.
He tied his shoelaces.
He was barefoot.

*

At the time, he was seeing
a Scandinavian woman
whose life was her watercolours:
orange skies, pink highways.
She wanted to live in a cave
and win the Nobel Prize.
I'm not interested
in saving the world, he told her,
it's hard enough remembering
to change my underpants.

*

Then he wrote a story
about a bad writer
and thirty-seven people
sent him insulting letters:
How dare he portray them
in such a callous manner?
He couldn't even remember
meeting fourteen of them.
Three or four of them
were actually good writers.

Geoff Hattersley

One Day, Her Father

cups a dying bird,
tries to revive it in front of the fire.

Outside, a shabby crowd of town sparrows
gathering on chimneys and washing-lines;
a tear in the mesh her father must mend
to protect the bright, darting canaries.

People pass the house as usual.

Her grandmother won't have birds inside,
they're unlucky, even on wallpaper.

She draws birds at school for others
but they get her anyway,
for her hat, her shoes, and everything else,

they hold her under at the baths,
drag her through rusting wire in the back-lane.
They gather round,
press their faces close

then leave her to the lonely afternoon.
The sound of someone's pigeons
like water boiling.
She waits among the huts till dark.

People pass the cutting as usual.

A stray feather spirals, lands in her palm.
Somewhere, in the distance, her father calls.

Jeanette Hattersley

Crossing Point

Everything was new:
her coat heavy as winter;
the boys' short trousers;
their shoes shining like ice.

Everything was new. The train
had wrenched her from Vienna –
Raindorfgasse that still held
the sheen of her childhood;
from loved faces with hope
bandaged tightly over worry,
from the thin waving of hands.

The station at Emmerich was new too:
concrete pillars straddling arches;
platforms spotless as German Maidens;
the strut of uniformed legs.

The red J stamped
in the corner of her passport
branded her cheeks long before
the compartment door was opened.

'You and your two children step down.'
The air smelt of fear
and as the train moved on,
the few miles to Holland
became infinity.

Her knees threatened to unhinge
when the boys were prised
out of her sight to be searched.
The control she'd built for months,
queueing to beg permits from clerks
ungiving as grilles, collapsed.

'Don't take them!' She sobbed.
Didn't see the unmalicious,
bovine eyes, the boots hoofing
in embarrassment. In her bag
one set of papers was out of date.
In her head the Fuehrer's words
fired and fired.

A woman checked the body
inside her coat, unlaced
her shoes. She was held
in a cold swing of terror.

The children returned intact.

It was dark when the train
pulled out, passed rows
of windows dimmed for war.
She knew they'd crossed
the border when light splashed
from every farm. Relief swept
like sun over greening fields
fenceless to the sky.

Myra Schneider

Change of State

She asks if she must buy them
with her pocket-money. Her voice is white.
The contours of her cotton blouse
quiver in the stillness of the air.

She's the fourth girl in Miss Ryder's class
to wonder, find a corner,
confirm her womanhood. In algebra
their eyes exchange, grow wise

while classmates search for x.
Sentries at the special times,
their whispers, full of secrets,
echo from the plain white tiles.

She stores them in a shoebox
that her brothers will not find.
The house is loud with silences
that burst at the closing of a door.

In mirrors, at odd angles,
in certain shades of light,
I mistake her for her mother,
and wonder if her thirteen years

will build a different pattern
as they creep to forty-two. She swings
on high heels round the corner,
chin thrust blind into the dark.

John Latham

The Kiss

'Go down to the room and kiss him,
There's not much left o' him in the bed.
He had a good run of it, over eighty years.
In a few days he'll be dead.'

My nine years shook at the words 'kiss him'.
I knew the old man was something to my father.
I knew I had to do what my father said.
I trembled to the bedroom door

And entered the room where the drawn curtains
Foiled the light.
Jack Boland was a white wreck on the pillows,
His body a slight

Hump under the eiderdown quilt, starred white and red,
Everything under the black crucifix
With gaping mouth and bleeding head.
He saw me, half-lifted a hand. 'Here, boy,' he said.

I walked across the bedroom floor
And felt the ice in his hands enter mine.
His eyes were screwed up with sickness, his hair was wet,
His tongue hung, slapped back. Every bone

In my body chilled as I bent my head
To the smell and feel of the sickspittle on his lips.
I kissed him, I find it hard to say what I kissed
But I drank him into me when I kissed him.

I recognised something of what in him was ending,
Of what in me had scarcely begun.
He seemed without fear, I think I gave him nothing,
He told me something of what it is to be alone.

There is no way to say good-bye to the dying.
Jack Boland said 'G'wan, boy! Go now.'
I shivered away from his hands, his smell,
The wet blobs of pain on hair and brow,

The weak, eager touch. My childfear
Went with me out into the corridor, stayed
Inside me till I stood again at my father's side,
Head down, thinking I was no longer afraid

Yet feeling still the deathlips rummaging at my lips,
The breath a sick warmth mingling with my breath.
It's thirty years since I bent my head to the kiss.
Ten thirties would not make me forget.

Brendan Kennelly

Scrubbing the Furious Walls of Mikuyu

Is this where they dump those rebels,
these haggard cells stinking of bucket
shit and vomit and the acrid urine of
yesteryears? Who would have thought I
would be gazing at these dusty, cobweb
ceilings of Mikuyu Prison, scrubbing
briny walls and riddling out impetuous
scratches of another dung-beetle locked
up before me here? Violent human palms
wounded these blood-bloated mosquitoes
and bugs (to survive), leaving these vicious
red marks. Monstrous flying cockroaches
crashed here. Up there the cobwebs trapped
dead bumblebees. Where did black wasps
get clay to build nests in this corner?

But here, scratches, insolent scratches!
I have marvelled at the rock paintings
of Mphunzi Hills once but these grooves
and notches on the walls of Mikuyu Prison,
how furious, what barbarous squiggles!
How long did this anger languish without
charge without trial without visit here and
what justice committed? This is the moment
we dreaded; when we'd all descend into
the pit, alone; without a wife or a child
without mother; without paper or pencil
without a story (just three Bibles for
ninety men) without charge without trial.
This is the moment I never needed to see.

Shall I scrub these brave squiggles out
of human memory then or should I perhaps
superimpose my own, less caustic; dare I
overwrite this precious scrawl? Who'd
have known I'd find another prey without
charge without trial (without bitterness)
in these otherwise blank walls of Mikuyu
Prison? No, I will throw my water and mop
elsewhere. We have liquidated too many
brave names out of the nation's memory;
I will not rub out another nor inscribe
my own, more ignoble, to consummate this
moment of truth I have always feared!

Jack Mapanje

Love in a Bathtub

Years later we'll remember the bathtub,
the position
          of the taps
the water, slippery
as if a bucketful
          of eels had joined us...
we'll be old, our children grown up
but we'll remember the water
                    sloshing out
the useless soap,
the mountain of wet towels.
'Remember the bathtub in Belfast?'
we'll prod each other –

Sujata Bhatt

In Doubt

Best of my books, I have never read it,
Only from dream to dream gathered
That somewhere it had appeared —
Pirated, decades ago,
Verse or prose picked up
By someone wiser than I from work I'd mislaid, forgotten.

On my own shelves I have found a copy,
The cover so faded,
The title so rubbed that barely I could make out:
DIARY OF THE GODFATHERED. Not mine! Not mine!
But the name was above it, in durable type.

Never now I shall read it.
Posthumous from the start,
It was always beyond me,
Its coherence that of the dark,
Its light not that I can see by
But unbroken, undiffused.

Let it slip again into lostness
Behind recognizable spines.

Michael Hamburger

Going Westwards

I go westwards in the Desert
with my shame on my shoulders,
that I was made a laughing-stock
since I was as my people were.

Love and the greater error,
deceiving honour spoiled me,
with a film of weakness on my vision,
squinting at mankind's extremity.

Far from me the Island
when the moon rises on Quattara,
far from me the Pine Headland
when the morning ruddiness is on the Desert.

Camus Alba is far from me
and so is the bondage of Europe,
far from me in the North-West
the most beautiful grey-blue eyes.

Far from me the Island
and every loved image in Scotland,
there is a foreign sand in History
spoiling the machines of the mind.

Far from me Belsen and Dachau,
Rotterdam, the Clyde and Prague,
and Dimitrov before a court
hitting fear with the thump of his laugh.

Guernica itself is very far
from the innocent corpses of the Nazis,
who are lying in the gravel
and in the khaki sand of the Desert.

There is no rancour in my heart
against the hardy soldiers of the Enemy,
but the kinship that there is among
men in prison on a tidal rock

waiting for the sea flowing
and making cold the warm stone;
and the coldness of life (is)
in the hot sun of the Desert.

But this is the struggle not to be avoided,
the sore extreme of human-kind,
and though I do not hate Rommel's army
the brain's eye is not squinting.

And be what was as it was,
I am of the big men of Braes,
of the heroic Raasay MacLeods,
of the sharp-sword Mathesons of Lochalsh;
and the men of my name – who were braver
when their ruinous pride was kindled?

Sorley MacLean

The Fifth

Aldeburgh Poetry Festival

5 – 7 November 1993

Wendy Cope
Philip Gross
Elizabeth Jennings
Vyacheslav Kupriyanov
Ivan V. Lalíc
Wes Magee
Elma Mitchell
Dennis O'Driscoll
Sheenagh Pugh
David Scott
Peter Scupham
Jo Shapcott
Iain Crichton Smith
Julio Valle-Castillo
Susan Wicks

My Country

Jumping Jack

This is the wild one
    (LOOK OUT!)
unpredictable
as Brian Clough
    (CAREFUL!)
and a real eater
of toes.

It goes mad
at a lick of flame
    (STAND BACK!)
and is a distant cousin
    (WATCH IT!)
of the Mercurian
glass-hopper.

Like a crackle
of rifle fire
    (IT'S COMING!)
it leaps, leaps
through the night
    (RUN! RUN!)
seeking you out.

Scatter!
Run!

It's got the scent
of your
Wellington Boots!

Wes Magee

Branches

I saw my father and mother standing
in a pond, against sunlight on rushes,
my mother's thin arm reaching
from between the small suns of water-lilies,
and saw that a spider
had strung threads from my father's knees
to glitter out over the water;
that their bleached bones had hardened
in the green on green of circles
and the paired blue wings of dragonflies,
the minute dance of egg-laying.
And I was glad
that they still stood there, sun-dry and reaching,
and I was grateful
that no-one had needed to bury them,
shut them out of all that light.

Susan Wicks

Goat

Dusk, deserted road, and suddenly
I was a goat. To be truthful, it took
two minutes, though it seemed sudden,
for the horns to pop out of my skull,
for the spine to revolutionize and go
horizontal, for the fingers to glue
together and for the nails to become
important enough to upgrade to hoof.
The road was not deserted any more, but full
of goats, and I liked that, even though I hate
the rush hour on the tube, the press of bodies.
Now I loved snuffling behind his or her ear,
licking a flank or two, licking and snuffling here,
there, wherever I liked. I lived for the push
of goat muscle and goat bone, the smell of goat fur,
goat breath and goat sex. I ended up on the edge
of the crowd where the road met the high
hedgerow with the scent of earth, a thousand
kinds of grass, leaves and twigs, flower-heads
and the intoxicating tang of the odd ring-pull
or rubber to spice the mixture. I wanted
to eat everything. I could have eaten the world
and closed my eyes to nibble at the high
sweet leaves against the sunset. I tasted
that old sun and the few dark clouds
and some tall buildings far away in the next town.
I think I must have swallowed an office block
because this grinding enormous digestion tells me
it's stuck on an empty corridor which has
at the far end, I know, a tiny human figure.

Jo Shapcott

A Classroom

The day was wide and that whole room was wide,
The sun slanting across the desks, the dust
Of chalk rising. I was listening
As if for the first time,
As if I'd never heard our tongue before,
As if a music came alive for me.
And so it did upon the lift of language,
A battle poem, *Lepanto*. In my blood
The high call stirred and brimmed.
I was possessed yet coming for the first
Time into my own
Country of green and sunlight,
Place of harvest and waiting
Where the corn would never all be garnered but
Leave in the sun always at least one swathe.
So from a battle I learnt this healing peace,
Language a spell over the hungry dreams,
A password and a key. That day is still
Locked in my mind. When poetry is spoken
That door is opened and the light is shed,
The gold of language tongued and minted fresh.
And later I began to use my words,
Stared into verse within that class-room and
Was called at last only by kind inquiry
'How old are you?' 'Thirteen'
'You are a thinker'. More than thought it was
That caught me up excited, charged and changed,
Made ready for the next fine spell of words,
Locked into language with a golden key.

Elizabeth Jennings

The Duke of Nowhere

I was the son of the Duke of Nowhere.
Nowhere was home. The first sound I remember

was engines sawing steam, the butt
and squeal of waggons full of clunk

shunted cruelly. Lifted to the window-sill
I had my first sight of our exile

as I thought: *Here, me,*
watching. There, trains, going away.

*

He was living incognito
but his secret was safe with me.

I was the solitary heir to everything
he never once mentioned. I guessed,

from his brooding, his whole silent days,
it must be vast. The lost estates

grew vaster in the weeks,
then months, he went away and stayed.

*

Beyond the roofs, beyond the dockyard wall
were cranes, then the edge of the world.

On a clear day I could watch grey frigates
climb it and slip over. I woke one night

to singing in the streets that suddenly
grew small as all the hooters of the fleet

brawled up together, blurring
Home... as if any such place

existed, over the horizon, anywhere.

Philip Gross

The Last Wolf In Scotland

I am a wolf. I know this
from way back, when my mother's
hot tongue prickled over the heap
that was me and the others,
as she whispered: *wolf wolf wolf wolf.*

There are four kinds: wolf,
not-wolf, wolf-food and hurt-wolf.
Not-wolf does nothing to the world;
wolf-food is warm, floods your throat,
fills your guts with sleep. Hurt-wolf
stiffens hairs, sharpens eyes and ears,
thumps inside you.

Wolf smelled different
from the world. When I was blind,
all the dark smelled of wolf; later
we blinked our way into a dazzle
of smells: a music, note overlaying
note, but always the deep one
under all.

The other day
I went to drink, and wolf
looked up at me. I'd forgotten
the face. So long since I touched
wolf. I used to find
tracks sometimes, or fancy I heard
a call at full moon. Never near.

I miss that smell, the gap
in the pattern, the note I can't hear
in the music. I miss fur and tongues
and singing voices. I miss the piece
that fell out of the world.

Sheenagh Pugh

PLAYING FOR ENGLAND

He sat by the boot shop window
fettling the studs for Saturday's match,
his apron slashed almost to shreds.
As farm carts bounced back from the fields
he thought of the new schoolteacher,
and the match. The Match.
It kept coming back to that.

The lasts, the knife, and the needle
were set aside for the weekend
so he could scrummage with unaccustomed
other shoulders. He left the last shoe
to be mended, with the thread dangling.

Chosen to play for England
in the year of the General Strike
he shook the hand of George V
at Twickenham. His white strip engaging
the king's black overcoat and bowler.

Rose on the chest, buttons and collar;
full, pocketed shorts; bandage garters;
dubbin and embrocation.
The rest was himself:
solid, neckless Cumberland.

The match was the usual mixture
of dread and exultation, cracking of heads,
snotting out of one nostril.
He gum-shielded his half-time orange
and on his hunkers took in the tactics.
The scrum steamed as the light dwindled.

Feeding out the notched leather strap
for letting the window down of the last train
he was the only one to alight:
tasselled, velvet cap in the bag.
London was a single bird's song away.

They lost, but never mind.
There was the home ground
looking up to the mountains;
the schoolteacher encouraging
her African violets; and round about
the folks' shoes to make and mend.

David Scott

This Poem…

This poem is dangerous: it should not be left
Within the reach of children, or even of adults
Who might swallow it whole, with possibly
Undesirable side-effects. If you come across
An unattended, unidentified poem
In a public place, do not attempt to tackle it
Yourself. Send it (preferably, in a sealed container)
To the nearest centre of learning, where it will be rendered
Harmless, by experts. Even the simplest poem
May destroy your immunity to human emotions.
All poems must carry a Government warning. Words
Can seriously affect your heart.

Elma Mitchell

Rafaela Padilla

I was going to the clandestine hospital
by the old Phoenix Cinema in Masaya
to give serum to a combatant
wounded in the Retreat.
There the guards
smashed me like a clay pot
with kicks and blows from their rifle butts.
Over the college steps that afternoon
spread a pool of my blood
and my sleek black hair.

I still resist blows, death,
I mind not minding the sick,
leaving my children motherless.
Hospital workers, Doctors, Nurses,
Comrades: our ancient human pain
is new, different and untransferable
in every patient. Remember that.
Don't ever forget.

Julio Valle-Castillo

Going Out: Lancasters, 1944

'They're going out', she said.
  Together we watch them go,
The dark crossed on the dusk,
  The slow slide overhead

And the garden growing cold,
  Flowers bent into grey,
The fields of earth and sky
  Losing their strength to hold

The common lights of day
  Which warm our faces still.
Feet in the rustling grass
  We watch them pass away,

The heavy web of sound
  Catching at her throat.
We stand there hand-in-hand,
  Our steady, shifting ground

Spreading itself to sand,
  The crisp and shining sea.
Wave upon wave they go,
  And we stand hand-in-hand,

The slow slide overhead,
  Stitched on a roll of air,
As if they knew the way,
  As if they were not dead.

Peter Scupham

Places We Love

Places we love exist only through us,
Space destroyed is only illusion in the constancy of time,
Places we love we can never leave,
Places we love together, together, together,

And is this room really a room, or an embrace,
And what is beneath the window: a street or years?
And the window is only the imprint left by
The first rain we understood, returning endlessly,

And this wall does not define the room, but perhaps the night
Your son began to move in your sleeping blood,
A son like a butterfly of flame in your hall of mirrors,
The night you were frightened by your own light,

And this door leads into any afternoon
Which outlives it, forever peopled
With your casual movements, as you stepped,
Like fire into copper, into my only memory;

When you go, space closes over like water behind you,
Do not look back: there is nothing outside you,
Space is only time visible in a different way,
Places we love we can never leave.

Ivan V. Lalíc

NAMES

She was Eliza for a few weeks
When she was a baby –
Eliza Lily. Soon it changed to Lil.

Later she was Miss Steward in the baker's shop
And then 'my love', 'my darling', Mother.

Widowed at thirty, she went back to work
As Mrs Hand. Her daughter grew up,
Married and gave birth.

Now she was Nanna. 'Everybody
Calls me Nanna,' she would say to visitors.
And so they did – friends, tradesmen, the doctor.

In the geriatric ward
They used the patients' Christian names.
'Lil,' we said, 'or Nanna,'
But it wasn't in her file
And for those last bewildered weeks
She was Eliza once again.

Wendy Cope

Way of Life

The longest queues.
The cheapest cuts.

The high season beaches.
The rush hour delays.

The densely populated quarters.
The comprehensive schools.

The public ward for babies.
The public house for celebration.

The special offers.
The soccer turnstiles.

When admission was reduced.
When group rates were available.

During lunchtime or weekend.
During Sunday or bank holiday.

At weddings, parks, parades.
At Christmas markets, January sales.

Wherever people gathered.
When crowds took to the streets.

Dennis O'Driscoll

Report on an Angel

An angel was reported at thirteen-forty hours
in a locality not normally frequented by angels;
when captured, he offered no resistance:
such apathy on the part of an angel
is considered out of the question.
The angel's wingspan measured no less than
two metres ninety-eight centimetres;
with a weight of seventy-two kilograms,
flight with such wings is, according
to the laws of aerodynamics, impossible.
The white fabric of the angel's uniform
was synthetic in origin and non-hermetic,
presenting certain objections
to the angel's residence in space.
The angel categorically refused to speak
with representatives from the humanities,
as a result of which his speech was deemed non-articulate
and unfit for the communication of the divine will.
A search of the angel failed to reveal an identity card:
in other words, he had no proof of citizenship.
In natural and artificial light
the angel failed to produce a halo;
this was apparent to the naked eye, thus casting
a shadow on the imaginings of prominent painters.
The above data having ruled out the possibility
of the angel being of any interest to science,
and his further detention being held inexpedient
for the purposes of anti-religious propaganda,
the above-mentioned was duly released, whereupon
he melted into the sky at sixteen-thirty hours.

Vyacheslav Kupriyanov

That Island Formed You

That island formed you, its black-hatted men
and stony bibles. How your father's beard
streamed like a cataract. And the heart's devoured
by the black rays of a descending sun.
Always they're making fences, making barred
gates to keep the wind out, their slow pace
deliberate and punctual. Who has heard
of the terrible cyclones that infect deep space?
The daffodils are yellow on the wind
but in these souls where is the love, my dear,
to dally in fine leisure as the clear
smoke rises from the houses, and the cock
shrills redly from the waste abundant air?

Iain Crichton Smith

The Sixth

Aldeburgh Poetry Festival

4 – 6 November 1994

Beliefs

John Agard
John Burnside
Robert Etty
Vicki Feaver
Dana Gioia
John Harvey
Donna Hilbert
Selima Hill
Rutger Kopland
Frank Kuppner
Rhona McAdam
Roger McGough
Don Paterson
Meg Peacocke
Zsuzsa Rakovszky
Michael Rosen
Peter Sansom
Matthew Sweeney
Tamar Yoseloff

Hot Food

We sit down to eat
and the potato's a bit hot
so I only put a little bit on my fork
and I blow
whooph whooph
until it's cool
just cool
then into the mouth
nice.
And there's my brother
he's doing the same
whooph whooph
into the mouth
nice.
There's my mum
she's doing the same
whooph whooph
into the mouth
nice.

But my dad.
My dad.
What does he do?
He stuffs a great big chunk of potato
into his mouth.
Then
that really does it.
His eyes pop out
he flaps his hands
he blows, he puffs, he yells
he bobs his head up and down
he spits bits of potato
all over his plate
and he turns to us and he says,
'Watch out everybody –
the potato's very hot.'

Michael Rosen

Asleep In a Chair

Asleep in a chair for three hours?
Take that man away. Bind him
and bundle him into a mini-cab,
drive through the Southern English night
till you see the lights of Brighton,
then throw him out on the South Downs.

Hopefully it will be sub zero
and wet as Ireland. (*Drunk* and
asleep in a chair for three hours,
with the TV and the gas fire on?)
Pick a field with cattle in it,
or better still, a nervy horse.

Make sure there's no stream near,
or even a house. Get miles away
from a shop or a chemist —
empty out his pockets just in case.
Smash his glasses while you're at it.
Forget you liked him, lose his name.

Burn his shoes to ash beside him,
keep his jeans as a souvenir.
Cut his hair off (*all* his hair).
Asleep in a chair for three hours?
By the time you're finished, honey,
he might have learned to sleep in a bed.

Matthew Sweeney

Tango

Let us invent marble and five o'clock.
I'll take white, you take black.
How engagingly we rhyme
across the chequered level in the perfume
of tea and petits fours.

I shall sample the tiniest slice
of the Grand Succès on the lemon terrace,
the newly apparent moon
a delicacy cat-ice thin,
fresh as mimosa.

Your legs are dangerously long
under the palm trees at Menton,
my thighs all silk and hesitation
drawing the tango down
the polished length of the floor.

And the cellos have such slim waists
and violins are girls with flattened breasts.
Let us invent the chaise longue,
bamboo, Lapsang Souchong,
linen and panama.

You may cough and thump your stick,
but I have been up in the attic
and I have a bundle of postcards here to prove
that once we were seen to be in love
on the Riviera in nineteen twenty-four.

Meg Peacocke

Palm Tree King

Because I come from the West Indies
certain people in England seem to think
I is a expert on palm trees

So not wanting to sever dis link
with me native roots (know what ah mean?)
or to disappoint dese culture vulture
I does smile cool as seabreeze

and say to dem
which specimen
you interested in
cause you talking
to the right man
I is palm tree king
I know palm tree history
like de palm o me hand
In fact me navel string
bury under a palm tree

If you think de queen could wave
you ain't see nothing yet
till you see the Roystonea Regia
– that is the royal palm –
with she crown of leaves
waving calm-calm
over the blue Caribbean carpet
nearly 100 feet of royal highness

But let we get down to business
Tell me what you want to know
How tall a palm tree does grow?
What is the biggest coconut I ever see?
What is the average length of the leaf?

Don't expect me to be brief
cause palm tree history
is a long-long story
Anyway why you so interested
in length and circumference?
That kind of talk so ordinary
That don't touch the essence
of palm tree mystery
That is no challenge
to a palm tree historian like me

If you insist on statistics
why you don't pose a question
with some mathematical profundity?

Ask me something more tricky
like if a American tourist with a camera
take 9 minutes to climb a coconut tree
how long a English tourist without a camera
would take to climb the same coconut tree?

That is problem pardner
Now ah coming harder

If 6 straw hat
and half a dozen bikini
multiply by the same number of coconut tree
equal one postcard
how many square miles of straw hat
you need to make a tourist industry?

That is problem pardner
Find the solution
and you got a revolution

But before you say anything
let I palm tree king
give you dis warning
Ah want de answer in metric
it kind of rhyme with tropic
Besides it sound more exotic

John Agard

A Dream Mistaking a Person for What He Has Come to Represent

When Ted Hughes stayed at our house
he fried himself a full English breakfast
in a pan the size of a dustbin lid.
The pan had a case, like a guitar; and a strap
to strap it to his back like a busker.
But at that moment it was sizzling and roaring.
As was he, a strenuous chef, and too big
if truth be told for our galley-kitchen.

We were too shy to ask if any of those
sausages, bacon, eggs, mushrooms, fried bread and tomatoes
were for us. We are not vegetarian,
and we were hungry, and the larder and fridge
now empty. It is a wise man, he said at last,
settling himself at our breakfast bar
and making free with the brown sauce,
who owns his own frying pan.

Peter Sansom

The Doctor Book

I loved the big doctor book
with cut-away pictures
of the human body,
the highway map of arteries
and veins, intestines
like the snakes I made with clay,
the liver, so slimy and dark
I could almost feel it slip through my hand.
Best of all, I liked the pictures
of the smallpox victims,
their bodies almost absent
under a mass of festering sores.
My grandpa had smallpox when he was a boy,
but he recovered without a scar
to look like Gary Cooper.
If such a miracle were possible,
then surely I was safe in his house.

Donna Hilbert

The Myth of The Twin

Someone is still awake
in the night of my grandfather's house
with its curtains and potted palms
and its books full of beech leaves
pressed so the colours would stay,

and someone is having the dream
I had for weeks: out walking on the beach
I lifted a pebble and split it
open, like an apricot, to find
a live child hatched in the stone;

like radio, the whisper of the tide,
the feel of a pulse in the dark, when I stay up all night
and answers come, single and clear, like the calling of birds,
or the pull of the sea, when the moon sails high in the clouds
and I pick out the shapes on its surface: a handprint, an iris.

John Burnside

Lily Pond

Thinking of new ways to kill you
and bring you back from the dead,
I try drowning you in the lily pond –

holding your head down
until every bubble of breath
is squeezed from your lungs

and the flat leaves and spiky flowers
float over you like a wreath.
I sit on the stones until I'm numb,

until, among reflections of sky,
water-buttercups, spears of iris,
your face rises to the surface –

a face that was always puffy
and pale, so curiously unchanged.
A wind rocks the waxy flowers, curls

the edges of the leaves. Blue dragonflies
appear and vanish like ghosts.
I part the mats of yellow weed

and drag you to the bank, covering
your green algae-stained corpse
with a white sheet. Then, I lift the edge

and climb in underneath –
thumping your chest,
breathing into your mouth.

Vicki Feaver

Some Notes About A Hare

Profiled through brambles, it's more
like a woodcock: shut eye
pale, ear a neat
skull-stripe; it licks a paw,
surprisingly cattish, back
another molehill in the grass
that's fine-stalked like the Wyeth
of the girl who sits
as still as this hare,
now.
            Then the squeaks
of stock doves' flight,
mallards photo-finishing
and only the dipping, dark-
grey v of the ears of
a hare that knows how much its
life is worth;
                        and somewhere
this way, invisible,
a cooling dent in the grass.

Robert Etty

Chet Baker

looks out from his hotel room
across the Amstel to the girl
cycling by the canal who lifts
her hand and waves and when
she smiles he is back in times
when every Hollywood producer
wanted to turn his life
into that bitter-sweet story
where he falls badly, but only
in love with Pier Angeli,
Carol Lynley, Natalie Wood;
that day he strolled into
the studio, fall of fifty-two,
and played those perfect lines
across the chords of 'Funny Valentine'
and now when he looks from his window
and her passing smile up to the blue
of a perfect sky he knows
this is one of those rare days
when he can truly fly.

John Harvey

The Boston School of Cooking Cookbook

This is my mother's cookbook, its spine loose
with age, the fabric bare of colour at the seams
and weak, so it must be held tenderly, the way
my mother knows, easing into its pages
with her disobedient-knuckled hands.

This book is my mother's; she navigates
its mysteries with indifferent skill,
reads the runes of food-stains,
the faded trail of silverfish
who ate their random way over words;
she has the eye to decipher the tastes
of another time, scrawled
in the margins, invoking the power
of other kitchens, the fit of old aprons,
the shape of a family
swallowed into other lives.

This book's pages, furred with use
fade to brown. Its leaves have pressed
my mother's memories in perfect squares, the things
she needs concealed from time,
things she likes to come upon by chance:
household tips and obituaries, invitations
to weddings. My first poem is in there, and the card
someone made for mother's day. Sentiment
among the weeds of recipes she clipped
in more ambitious days
that crowd, untasted, between the even rows
of meals we chewed our way through
but never knew the names of, all those years
worth of peeled vegetables and trimmed meat,
a lifetime's preparation vanished
into our waiting mouths.

Rhona McAdam

In The Chelsea Physic Garden

To tell the truth, it's the names and not
the plants that get you, you thrill to Latin,
the 'icus' and 'atum', the beauty of endings.
I like the juicy berries of the belladonna,
the shoo-fly with its little maracas, all
the strange and unloved weeds. Growing up,
the lullabies my mother sang were about
lost love and how sad the past could be,
later. No Rock a Bye, Baby, just the facts.

Now, I love her for it, for the names
she gave me, collections of constellations,
varieties of sea shells, the flowers
we'd pick out walking, bring home to dry.
I used to save abandoned baby birds, frogs
from snake's jaws. It would always end
in tears. Forgive me, there are things I want
to say, but I have no words, just Proper
Names, more Latin, prosaic American slang.

In the fairy tale version, we are planted,
not side by side, as you might expect,
but in separate hemispheres, never to meet.
You the cool fern, adaptable to rainy climates,
and rain or shine, reliable. I'm the problem,
spiky, dangerous, the occasional flower,
poison of course. But exotic. Experts travel
miles to meet me. I dream of leaves, your
soft caress. I guess I'd slash you to bits.

Tamar Yoseloff

The Ferryman's Arms

About to sit down with my half-pint of Guinness
I was magnetized by a remote phosphorescence
and drawn, like a moth, to the darkened back room
where a pool-table hummed to itself in the corner.
With ten minutes to kill and the whole place deserted
I took myself on for the hell of it. Slotting
a coin in the tongue, I looked round for a cue –
while I stood with my back turned, the balls were deposited
with an abrupt intestinal rumble; a striplight
batted awake in its dusty green cowl.
When I set down the cue-ball inside the parched D
it clacked on the slate; the nap was so threadbare
I could screw back the globe, given somewhere to stand –
as physics itself becomes something negotiable
a rash of small miracles covers the shortfall:
I went on to make an immaculate clearance.
A low punch with a wee dab of side, and the black
did the vanishing trick while the white stopped
before gently rolling back as if nothing had happened,
shouldering its way through the unpotted colours.

The boat chugged up to the little stone jetty
without breaking the skin of the water, stretching,
as black as my stout, from somewhere unspeakable
to here, where the foaming lip mussitates endlessly,
trying, with a nutter's persistence, to read
and re-read the shoreline. I got aboard early,
remembering the ferry would leave on the hour
even for only my losing opponent;
but I left him there, stuck in his tent of light, sullenly
knocking the balls in, for practice, for next time.

Don Paterson

The Island

Men want to understand, and think they do,
and maybe if they don't it's not their fault,
but basically this place belongs to us.
We like to organise ourselves ourselves.
And anyway, anyone can visit —
brothers, fathers, lovers, anyone.
My son comes often; or I visit him.
You ask us if we miss them. Not at all.
We don't use cars, or electricity,
and men especially seem to find that hard.
Another thing — we feel healthier.
We work the horses; bear much fewer children;
and eat and dress and live very simply.
We shepherd sheep. We scale trees for fruit.
We abseil cliffs for samphire and fresh eggs;
and some of us, as you have pointed out,
migrating to the cities, abseil glass.

Selima Hill

Waiting-Room

This friendly room is like a well-meant
conspiracy or a hushed-up scandal,
with its slender vases, wide somnolent

chairs, and a pile of last year's glossy mags
on the crocheted tablecloth. Between dark
silhouettes of houseplants a few frayed rags

of sky are visible above the narrow street.
Our only clue is the picture of a faint
nude on the opposite wall, stretching before velvet

curtains – how enigmatic! – and how innocently
she hints at the bed within, at rubber gloves
and at the point where high technology

meets startled flesh. We watch each other, disciplined
and fully dressed: parading anxieties
like toy balloons that drift in a low wind.

Do I really want this? Am I free to want something else?
Or only this, these bittersweet crumbs,
clichés of tenderness, possessiveness?

These wars of religion for ever bickering over
idols of flesh and blood? We are always using
each other's towels and toothbrushes, their

truths strangle my truths, at night I hear them
at arm's length, breathing to rhythms
alien to mine, while the flotsam and jetsam

of the world accumulates in me, heavy as salt,
I'm becoming opaque – do I want to feel
so much, in such a haphazard fashion, and all

for nothing? Or should I remain, a sheet of virgin
glass, a frozen possibility, behind which time
catches fire, my time – later, later again.

Zsuzsa Rakovszky

CINDERS

After the pantomime, carrying you back to the car
On the coldest night of the year
My coat, black leather, cracking in the wind.

Through the darkness we are guided by a star
It is the one the Good Fairy gave you
You clutch it tightly, your magic wand.

And I clutch you tightly for fear you blow away
For fear you grow up too soon and – suddenly,
I almost slip, so take it steady down the hill.

Hunched against the wind and hobbling
I could be mistaken for your grandfather
And sensing this, I hold you tighter still.

Knowing that I will never see you dressed for the Ball
Be on hand to warn you against Prince Charmings
And the happy ever afters of pantomime.

On reaching the car I put you into the baby seat
And fumble with straps I have yet to master
Thinking, if only there were more time. More time.

You are crying now. Where is your wand?
Oh no. I can't face going back for it
Let some kid find it in tomorrow's snow.

Waiting in the wings, the witching hour.
Already the car is changing. Smells sweet
Of ripening seed. We must go. Must go.

Roger McGough

from: Last Eternal Moments

13

Truly, in the four-fifths of an eternity
in which hydrogen, its derivatives and its predecessors
have whistled outwards, combining and recombining;
in the billions of years in which chaotic gases and liquids
gave the earth innumerable unseen surfaces;
in the unimaginable tempests of the unimportant sun;
in the slow drift of unsuspected vibrant species to land;
in the huge rock-crystals that hurl negligently past nearby;
in the tiny crystals which can change us utterly;
in the inextinguishable heat which shrieks and rampages
somewhere away beneath that most elegant footwear
discarded beside a bed, upon which a woman
lies, laughing, as she reads out something absurd from a magazine –
so devastating a complex pattern of simple sounds –
that this shy hill, whose crest we help to populate
is instantly revealed to be the living centre
of Time and History and Joy and Musicality –
and Something Else even greater – what is it called?
Oh, keep talking; keep talking until I can remember.
Another four-fifths of a second should be all I need.

Frank Kuppner

The Valley

1

You see us again sitting in the grass;
those faces of ours, looking
as though they were seeing something
that makes them extraordinarily happy,

like the faces of the blind, unaware
of how they are seen, unsuspecting, looking
at their own secret.

In my notes you read very little
of this, I simply wrote:
been to the valley again, looked a long time,
it was still there.

2

And then you see again what
we were sitting looking at:
grey edge of the wood, the wickerwork
fencing drenched in twilight,
about us the very slightly undulating
soft-green meadows and in the hollow
the little row of spindly alders straying
along the invisible stream.

Then this is what must have made us
so extraordinarily happy.

3

You see how often these photographs have been
looked at, how often, too, the slip of paper
has been read, on which was written it was still there,
how spotted and thumb-marked they are.

That whole perfect world that must be
there – the wholly undiscoverable answer
to the question which world that is.

Rutger Kopland

Planting a Sequoia

All afternoon my brothers and I have worked in the orchard,
Digging this hole, laying you into it, carefully packing the soil.
Rain blackened the horizon, but cold winds kept it over the Pacific,
And the sky above us stayed the dull gray
Of an old year coming to an end.

In Sicily a father plants a tree to celebrate his first son's birth –
An olive or a fig tree – a sign that the earth has one more life to bear.
I would have done the same, proudly laying new stock into my father's
 orchard,
A green sapling rising among the twisted apple boughs,
A promise of new fruit in other autumns.

But today we kneel in the cold planting you, our native giant,
Defying the practical custom of our fathers,
Wrapping in your roots a lock of hair, a piece of an infant's birth cord,
All that remains above earth of a first-born son,
A few stray atoms brought back to the elements.

We will give you what we can – our labor and our soil,
Water drawn from the earth when the skies fail,
Nights scented with the ocean fog, days softened by the circuit of
 bees.
We plant you in the corner of the grove, bathed in western light,
A slender shoot against the sunset.

And when our family is no more, all of his unborn brothers dead,
Every niece and nephew scattered, the house torn down,
His mother's beauty ashes in the air,
I want you to stand among strangers, all young and ephemeral to you,
Silently keeping the secret of your birth.

Dana Gioia

The Seventh

Aldeburgh Poetry Festival

3 – 5 November 1995

Risks

Peter Bland
Charles Boyle
Ian Duhig
Lauris Edmond
Nigel Jenkins
P. J. Kavanagh
Tom Leonard
Thomas Lynch
John Lyons
Paula Meehan
Adrian Mitchell
Dorothy Nimmo
Deryn Rees-Jones
Norman Silver
Eira Stenberg
Sue Stewart
Grete Tartler
Gerard Woodward

Unrelated Incidents (3)

this is thi
six a clock
news thi
man said n
thi reason
a talk wia
BBC accent
iz coz yi
widny wahnt
mi ti talk
aboot thi
trooth wia
voice lik
wanna yoo
scruff. if
a toktaboot
thi trooth
lik wanna yoo
scruff yi
widny thingk
it wuz troo.
jist wanna yoo
scruff tokn.
thirza right
way ti spell
ana right way
ti tok it. this
is me tokn yir
right way a
spellin. this
is ma trooth.
yooz doant no
thi trooth
yirsellz cawz
yi canny talk
right, this is
the six a clock
nyooz. belt up.

Tom Leonard

Bluebells

The bluebells have other ideas
waking limp from their pointed dream,
the analysis of vases.

Their ragged tint is more telling
than the restless prose I wrap them in,
comforting each one
as I snip its sticky fuse

stretching the flora like fingertips
to the east and west of windows,
frayed lips easing down
to kiss the sill.

They crave the teapot,
a larger pool to lean from
where tannin homely as loam
fosters their lilac sheaf

my kitchen's bulb
warming the surface
as a sun might.

Sue Stewart

After the Deafening

You write me letters
Even though I'm still with you.
Our ears, clumsy

Treble clefs, just overwrought
Ornaments of flesh, now,
Since those local disasters.

And all our surviving neighbours
Share this visible world
Where men drive nails

Home with kisses, missing
The birds' traffic of whereabouts,
Their melodious debate

On the ownership of trees.
Even history's rendered harmless,
Its wars just airy turbulence;

Krakatoa's red mime,
Nagasaki's dazzling silence
That leaves its ring of deaf,

Like us, these are things
To fall asleep to, the shifting
Of midnight husbands,

The world making itself comfortable.
Our screams come out as
Nothing more than an arm's length of breath

That doesn't even wake us.
Even though you are next to me
I write you letters.

Gerard Woodward

Hymns Ancient and Modern

On a rough night spinning past
the macrocarpas' violent shadows
wind wrenched the car sideways
till for very apprehension I began singing
the purposeful hymns of childhood
All Hail the Power   O Worship the King
Su-un of my So-oul Thou Sa-aviour Dear

mist sent its wraiths whirling
queerly over the farms as I intoned
Rock of Ages, even at last Lest We Forget
(oh the smell of chrysanthemums
on terrible Anzac Days!).

But truly on Tinakori Hill
the dark spurs motioned me past
and I came on home. Up steps to the windy door
key in the lock   the first light switch
mail in a pile on the table
your letter.

'It happened last week, in England.
The children have been told.'
Six-year-old Josie, died of a brain tumour.
A small child, pretty, inclined to giggle
– that's really all I know.
How silent the wind is
it has no voice now
no song. It is just wind, after all
just air
the cruel and stupid air that will always
come and go at random –

in All Saints Sunday School
at a death we sang Abide With Me
in our effortless thin voices
and looked out the window
savouring all the Sunday dinners
still to come.

Lauris Edmond

Two Boyfriends

One sends me Turkish delights
inscribed with love lyrics
and wrapped in pink ribbons.

The other rides a Kawasaki.

One has dreams with subtitles
and investigates psychic phenomena
with litmus paper and tweezers.

The other rides a Kawasaki.

One has telephoto eyes
for capturing the folk-dances of water
and the conversations of clouds.

The other rides a Kawasaki.

One eats only free-range fruit
and cries when he sees children
partying at McDonald's.

The other rides a Kawasaki.

One talks to God in his spare time
and knits him jumpers
and warm woolly hats.

The other rides a Kawasaki.

One believes that our two names
are written somewhere on a golden scroll
and that sex is meaningful.

The other rides a Kawasaki.

Norman Silver

Moggy At Grimma's

Fee fi fo fum and look at the plunge in Grimma's Arden.
Watch the slips! They're a bit properly.
The gag won't hurt you, he's a blood boggy.
Flat him. Bently! He won't fight, he's only breaking.
A gnashy noise. Brown, Pincer, brown!
The brass is blush and clamp, the bones are green.

See the clash? Under the breeds?
Goldsplishes and polyglots. Frigs.
All lippery. Mutes under the leaving.
It's all crud at the bottom. Woeful!
Be woeful, brawling, don't want to brumble,
you'll get all brat!

Grimma's mouse smell molish and purey.
The more's lippery. What's in the hubbub? Names,
sacks of pards, bluedo and pelicans.
When you get colder Grimma will play with you,
snappy fumblies, widdley-tinks, necks and sadders.
You can go worst because you're longest.

The cock kicks. Grimma binds up the cock
with her big clay. She grinds and grinds,
the cock goes knick-knock and the time goes BONG.

Meet your tickys up. Link up your silk.
It's in your very grown hug with the habits on.
How many habits? Gone, who, me. Oh suck
at all those hums! Fetch the weaver,
weep up the hums all sweet and sidey.

Up in the pilchard there are asps
in the blindfold mopples, huzzing in the blowers.
Wipe moreberries under the knotting.
This one's dead. Meet it up, bawling. And a mother!

Look how star you can be from here! Proud arrows
boating over the sills and alleys, folds and goods,
bright out to the freeside across the way.

Roamtime now. Say butterfly to Grimma, wailing.
Grieve her a miss, grieve her a shrug,
sun again moon! She bends by the floor and braves.
She braves and braves as Moggy thrives away.

Dorothy Nimmo

Castration

Cutting, they called it –
but for all
his noise there was no
blood, no visible hurt:

just some thing in him
halted, to change
a bull-calf to a steer.

It didn't hurt, they said
as they caught and threw them,
locked each scrotum
for a second
in the cutter's iron gums.

The next one was mine:
round the yard we
chased him, brought him
down – hooves flying –
in a slither of dung.

They sat him upright.
like a man for barbering.
and I felt
in the warmth of his purse
for the tubes.
They gave me the tongs
and with all the steel
of my arms I
squeezed them home.

They fetched me another,
said he hadn't felt a thing.
But I wouldn't play.
With all that sky-wide bawling –
        sound his throat
        was never made for –
some nerve in me was severed.
There were words about
that weren't to be trusted.

Nigel Jenkins

Breaking Siesta

We tip-toed from siesta,
past havens of under-tree shadows,
past our grey clean-neck hen
reddening in midday glare:
Beak open, it was ventilating,
sharp thorn of its tongue stilled;
wing feathers stretched like open fan
in a shallow basin of yard dirt.

We found the cool, dark under-house,
played at secrets: She told me
not to be afraid, it would not bite
if I touched it.
Then, in the fumbling dark
she showed my hand how.

Seconds later I broke free,
saw our leghorn yard cock
treading the grey clean-neck.

John Lyons

Lovesong to Captain James T. Kirk

Captain. I never thought we'd come to this,
but things being what they are, being adults,
stardate '94 it's best to make the best of it
and laugh. What's done is done. Perhaps
I'll start to call you Jim or Jamie, James...

No one was more shocked than me when I arrived
(*the lady doth protest*) to find
my bruised and rainy planet disappeared
and me, materialised and reconstructed
on board the Starship Enterprise, all 60s
with my lacquered bee-hive and my thigh-high
skirt in blue, my Doctor Marten's and my jeans
replaced by skin-tight boots
and scratchy blue-black nylons rippling-
up my less-than-perfect calves. Sulu
looked worried. Spock cocked up one eyebrow
enigmatically, branding my existence
perfectly illogical. How nice, I thought. His ears.
Uhura smiled of course, and fiddled
with her hair. *O James.* Truth is
I loved you even as a child...

O slick-black-panted wanderer holding
your belly in, your phaser gun
on stun, and eyes like Conference pears! You're not my type
but I undress you, and we fuck
and I forgive your pancake make-up and mascara,
the darker shadows painted round your eyes.
The lava-lamp goes up and down. We're
a strange unison. Politically
Mismatched. Our mutual friend
The Doc takes notes. *Go easy Bones!*
Scotty is beaming and shouts *Energise,*
and all of a sudden you remind me

of my dad, my brother and my mum,
my body rising like a shadow from the past
on top of you. As I press your arms behind your head
I drape my breasts so that you
brush my nipples gently with your lips almost
involuntarily as we boldly go. Come slowly, Captain,
and we do, with both our pairs of eyes tight closed.

Deryn Rees-Jones

Crawley Welcomes Careful Drivers

I'd have lived opposite the Esso garage, where they put
the tiger in your tank. I'd have had three aunts –
Alice, Joan and the other one, who married beneath her –
a Hornby train set, a yoyo, a tree house, a military badge.

An only child, I'd have been allowed to stay up to watch the news.
Sometimes I would have wondered if my parents were really
my parents, and would have imagined sailing to Rio
to find my true father and meeting him in the stock exchange,

easily the tallest man there. Until then, I'd have fished
for sticklebacks with Jeremy, my friend. His father, something
in insurance, would have smoked a pipe with a curvy stem.
And one night, having talked about it for weeks, Jeremy

would have gone and done it: next morning, the assistant pro
would have found the bank manager's Jaguar crashed into a tree
off the eighteenth fairway and, lying on the back seat, asleep.
apparently unharmed, the bank manager's lovely naked daughter.

Around that time, I'd have opted for geography and economics.
I'd have worried about God and checked every nook and cranny
for signs
of hereditary disease. Jeremy would have gone up to Oxford.
I'd have learnt how to foxtrot with his younger sister.

Charles Boyle

Two Family Snaps

1. *In a Council-House Backyard* (Circa 1925)

Here's mum modelling her Susan Lenglen gear
with the penny-a-week insurance man
looking amazed at this ripe
housewife in white silk stockings leaning
over the clothesline. Over

the fence the neighbours' kids
mime her poses. They wink and strut
waving their Great Exhibition mugs. Mum
was much admired by a neighbourhood
that knew a bit of class when they saw it.

Talent will out, they all said.
It never did, but the neighbours
still applauded - being more
than faithful to those of their own
who always made the most of their lot.

2. *Big Game* (Circa 1928)

Here's dad in Africa living it up
with a dead pig under his foot.
He's got a big cigar and an ever bigger gun.
All around him there's space
and hordes of naked black lasses.

Just the place for a Bradford lad
brought up on Wesley and smog.
No wonder he's enjoying himself
killing and screwing and making a profit.
When this was taken he was nearly forty.

Another few months and they shipped him home
to work on the ledgers. He packed life up
but took another twenty years to drop off.
I'm looking at an Empire in its hey-day.
Even the dead pig is laughing.

Peter Bland

From the Irish

According to Dineen, a Gael unsurpassed
in lexicographical enterprise, the Irish
for moon means 'the white circle in a slice
of half-boiled potato or turnip'. A star
is the mark on the forehead of a beast
and the sun is the bottom of a lake, or well.

Well, if I say to you your face
is like a slice of half-boiled turnip,
your hair is the colour of a lake's bottom
and at the centre of each of your eyes
is the mark of the beast, it is because
I want to love you properly, according to Dineen.

Ian Duhig

The Wonders of the World

Tell me about the wonders of the world: a glow-worm
which feeds on earth
but never eats its fill
for fear that all the earth will be eaten up.
And think of those who sell themselves to death:
the mercenaries.
(But what a difference between 'ray' and 'raid':
for a moment you're frightened.)
And once in summer there was a swirl of schoolboys
in red blazers on the stone steps
with a scent of lime-trees over the scent of damp,
and weeds, jasmine, garden gnomes,
peasant women with wide straw hats making a ring of shade
like a space for prayer.
Or think of the cricket who sheds his skin
(the way you found him in the doorway)
before he begins to sing.
If you're hungry for wonders, stuff yourself with these
while they've not yet disappeared under a scab of grass,
while among them words too can flash like lightning.
Perhaps you will remember
these moments of gluttony
in the future, when you're asked 'Who –
your parents, your child, your great love, who –
taught you that poetry was where to look
for your ultimate salvation?'

Grete Tartler

News from Gloucestershire

This snow, thaw, frost, thaw and rain
Has bitten great gaps in the old limestone
Walls that summer visitors delighted in:
Dark grey, with rusty orange and sky-grey lichen
And mosses green as cress; they caught the sun
Pink in the morning and, white under the moon,
Shadowed the fox. They have fallen down,

Nor will be, nor should be, built again,
Fences being cheaper; they are done
That were my passion. Foxes' navigation, weasels' run,
Skilful catchers of every light, they open
Like graves, a jumble of yellow bone
That tractors tidy away. Visitors from the town
May vaguely remark an absence, travel on.

The thud, thud, is fence-posts going in.

P. J. Kavanagh

A Puppy Called Puberty

It was like keeping a puppy in your underpants
A secret puppy you weren't allowed to show to anyone
Not even your best friend or your worst enemy

You wanted to pat him stroke him cuddle him
All the time but you weren't supposed to touch him

He only slept for five minutes at a time
Then he'd suddenly perk up his head
In the middle of school medical inspection
And always on bus rides
So you had to climb down from the upper deck
All bent double to smuggle the puppy off the bus
Without the buxom conductress spotting
Your wicked and ticketless stowaway.

Jumping up, wet-nosed, eagerly wagging –
He only stopped being a nuisance
When you were alone together
Pretending to be doing your homework
But really gazing at each other
Through hot and hazy daydreams

Of those beautiful schoolgirls on the bus
With kittens bouncing in their sweaters.

Adrian Mitchell

Would You Jump Into My Grave As Quick?

'Would you jump into my grave as quick?'
my granny would ask when one of us took
her chair by the fire. You, woman,
done up to the nines, red lips a come on,
your breath reeking of drink
and your black eye on my man tonight
in a Dublin bar, think
first of the steep drop, the six dark feet.

Paula Meehan

from: The Eighth Day of the Week

1

It's hotter today than skin, a hundred in the shade.
I'm mixed up in a crime.
It's my task to find out who the murderer is
that's holding the family in terror.

She's a way of striking secretly,
kills child after child.
She has a sign
that shows her presence:
a pile of twigs appears on the oven,
and the next one knows
her turn has come.

When all the other children have been killed
and I alone am left,
I suddenly see the sign, the twigs.

Mummy's coming towards me,
feeling affectionate,
wanting to cuddle me in her lap
and promising protection.
I give her a look
and say I know
who the murderer is
and she won't succeed with me.

Eira Stenberg

Skating with Heather Grace

Apart from the apparent values,
there are lessons in the circular:
paradigms for history,
time in a round world, turning,
love with another of your species –

To watch my only daughter
widening her circles is to ease
headlong into the traffic
of her upbringing.

Until nearly four she screamed
at my absence, mourned
my going out for any reason,
cried at scoldings,
agreed to common lies regarding
thunder, Christmas,
baby teeth. Last year

she started school
without incident;
this year ballet and new math. Soon

I think my love will seem
entirely deficient.

Later there's the hokey-pokey
and dim lights for the partners' dance.
She finds a shaky nine-year-old
to skate around
in counter-clockwise orbits,
laughing.

Is it more willingness than balance?
Is letting go the thing that keeps her steady?

I lean against the side-boards sipping
coffee. I keep a smile ready.

Thomas Lynch

The Eighth

Aldeburgh Poetry Festival

1 – 3 November 1996

Trust & Betrayal

Fleur Adcock
Robert Crawford
Nuala Ní Dhomhnaill
Jane Duran
Peter Finch
Duncan Forbes
Stephen Knight
Gwyneth Lewis
Sharon Olds
Brian Patten
Patricia Pogson
Tadeusz Różewicz
Vernon Scannell
Charles Simic
Lemn Sissay
Hugo Williams

Flowers in the Kitchen

On buying her flowers
she said

‘There’s no food in the kitchen
and we can’t eat flowers’.

On buying her food
she said

‘You don’t buy flowers any more’.

Lemn Sissay

The Language Issue

I place my hope on the water
in this little boat
of the language, the way a body might put
an infant

in a basket of intertwined
iris leaves,
its underside proofed
with bitumen and pitch,

then set the whole thing down amidst
the sedge
and bulrushes by the edge
of a river

only to have it borne hither and thither,
not knowing where it might end up;
in the lap, perhaps,
of some Pharaoh's daughter.

Nuala Ní Dhomhnaill

The Tattoo

At the ferro-concrete bike sheds
I pass a love-note to Veronica.
I wear long trousers and Brylcreem now
but her only interest is proven prowess.
I tattoo her name on my arm in Quink
with a penknife and show her.
She is unimpressed.
She goes out with a big ted from the fifth
who pisses over bog doors when you're in there.
He wears knuckle-dusters and can make a noise like a fart
with his armpit. Everyone is scared.
At break the Head tells me
that only criminals and soldiers sport tattoos
and sends me home to remove it.
My mother refuses. There is a dispute.
Magnificently my photograph
appears in the paper. Schoolboy Banned.
Our family are resolute.

It is over when by mistake
I wash a week later
and the whole thing goes.
I return to school a hero
where after assembly Veronica smiles
and the big ted breaks my nose.

Peter Finch

The Surf Motel

Across the waves that vague, moss-covered knell
Drifting from The Surf Motel
's the dinner bell.

Starfish pack the car park at the height of every swell.

As always, every peal
Calls forth another conger eel
To nibble at the edges of the evening meal.

Silt and seaweed feast upon the carpets they conceal.

All evening, cleaners bail
Black water out of poky rooms to no avail –
Their patience and their buckets fail.

In hoover bags, like escapologists, fish flail

But still,
While tides will ruin everyone they fill,
Visitors remain for weeks, for years perhaps, until; until.

The cost of staying blurs on every bill.

Stephen Knight

Against Coupling

I write in praise of the solitary act:
of not feeling a trespassing tongue
forced into one's mouth, one's breath
smothered, nipples crushed against the
ribcage, and that metallic tingling
in the chin set off by a certain odd nerve:
unpleasure. Just to avoid those eyes would help –
such eyes as a young girl draws life from,
listening to the vegetal
rustle within her, as his gaze
stirs polypal fronds in the obscure
sea-bed of her body, and her own eyes blur.

There is much to be said for abandoning
this no longer novel exercise –
for not 'participating in
a total experience' – when
one feels like the lady in Leeds who
had seen *The Sound of Music* eighty-six times;

or more, perhaps, like the school drama mistress
producing *A Midsummer Night's Dream*
for the seventh year running, with
yet another cast from 5B.
Pyramus and Thisbe are dead, but
the hole in the wall can still be troublesome.

I advise you, then, to embrace it without
encumbrance. No need to set the scene,
dress up (or undress), make speeches.
Five minutes of solitude are
enough – in the bath, or to fill
that gap between the Sunday papers and lunch.

Fleur Adcock

Life

To begin with, things hardly changed.
Tentative spiders started to inch
their webs a little wider, sills
collected a litter of tiny flies,
a moth dusted a few cushions,
softened into the carpet.

The post slid through the brass box
with a fussy click
sifted into an untidy hill
all queries and demands unanswered.
Geraniums strained towards the light,
growing lopsided, dry.

The Cyclops opposite the sofa
stared unblinking. Only the fridge
shuddered from time to time.
Brown beetles pushed yellow dust
from holes in the spare room bookcase,
woodlice multiplied in the vegetable basket.

A pair of oranges hardened
on the larder shelf, while upstairs
an earwig settled in the soapdish
and in the bedroom, tucked up
in a floral duvet, the blackening carcass
pulsed gently with maggots.

Patricia Pogson

When I Grow Up

When I grow up I want to have a bad leg.
I want to limp down the street I live in
without knowing where I am. I want the disease
where you put your hand on your hip
and lean forward slightly, groaning to yourself.

If a little boy asks me the way
I'll try and touch him between the legs.
What a dirty old man I'm going to be when I grow up!
What shall we do with me?

I promise I'll be good
if you let me fall over in the street
and lie there calling like a baby bird. Please,
nobody come. I'm perfectly all right. I like it here.

I wonder would it be possible
to get me into a National Health Hospice
somewhere in Manchester?
I'll stand in the middle of my cubicle
holding onto a piece of string for safety,
shaking like a leaf at the thought of my suitcase.

I'd certainly like to have a nervous tic
so I can purse my lips up all the time
like Cecil Beaton. Can I be completely bald, please?
I love the smell of old pee.
Why can't I smell like that?

When I grow up I want a thin piece of steel
inserted into my penis for some reason.
Nobody's to tell me why it's there. I want to guess!
Tell me, is that a bottle of old Burgundy
under my bed? I never can tell
if I feel randy any more, can you?

I think it's only fair that I should be allowed
to cough up a bit of blood when I feel like it.
My daughter will bring me a special air cushion
to hold me upright and I'll watch
in baffled admiration as she blows it up for me.

Here's my list: nappies, story books, munchies,
something else. What was the other thing?
I can't remember exactly,
but when I grow up I'll know. When I grow up
I'll pluck at my bedclothes to collect lost thoughts.
I'll roll them into balls and swallow them.

Hugo Williams

The Stars

My mother thought the tall, dark, handsome stranger
She married in the boy-next-door looked like
The 1950's film star, Stewart Granger.

Hoping it would rise to number one,
The only 45 she ever bought
Was *Dominique* by the Singing Nun.

And two years, is it, since my mother died?
Madame Tussaud's has melted Stewart Granger
And the Singing Nun's committed suicide.

Duncan Forbes

Braided Rug

The all America rag rug
I hide my feet in
twists as the Hudson
has learned to twist
outdoing its clouds
of dust. It opens out –
as the Missouri offers
in flood and mire
its alms,
or the Potomac pulls
at its raggedy banks.

It braids blue-grey
with river-black, silver
for the rare winter stillness
as if left out all night
by the mountains.
The repeated stopped waters
creak with my weight.

The floorboards of our kitchen
are polished to a nicety.
I am nimble on these knots.
I speak all the riverland tongues
of my mother tongue.
My accent fathers me.
My voice is too loud –
even the heron, the herring gull
disappear.

In the middle of London
I am elsewhere. To the long gone,
to the dead in me
I cry breathe now, breathe.
I know my bailiwick.
I stand on my rug.

Jane Duran

from: Six Poems on Nothing

IV

He started to transform himself in sixty-three,
though few of us knew it at the very start
or suspected his goal was transparency.

We only noticed that he'd disappear
from time to time off the factory floor.
We covered, but his absences grew longer

till, for all our lying, he was finally caught
by the foreman in the locker room,
tied up in a clear chrysalis of thought.

Nothing would shift him, so he got the sack,
but took it quite calmly. When I walked him home
he explained that there was no turning back

from his self-translation. The scales of a butterfly
aren't coloured at all, but are shingles of white
which simply accept the prismatics of light

in spectacular patterns. That humility
was what he was after. I met him often
and watched his skin's translucency

deepen with practice, so that his derm
and epidermis were transmogrified.
He was able to earn some cash on the side

as a medical specimen while muscles and veins
were still visible and then even more
for the major organs as he became pure

through his praying (this after his wife
had sued him for lack of comfort and joy
in their marriage) but by then his life

was simply reflective. I could only discern
his shape in the sunshine, so purged was he
of his heaviness and opacity.

He knew he was nothing. Through him I saw
colours shades deeper than ever before
and detail: the ratchets on a snail's rough tongue,

the way light bruises, how people fall
to weakness through beauty and when we came
to him for vision, he accepted us all,

made us more real, gave us ourselves
redeemed in the justice of his paraphrase,
the vivid compassion of his body's gaze.

Gwyneth Lewis

Popular Mechanics

The enormous engineering problems
You'll encounter by attempting to crucify yourself
Without helpers, pulleys, cogwheels,
And other clever mechanical contrivances –

In a small, bare, white room
With only a loose-legged chair
To reach the height of the ceiling –
Only a shoe to beat the nails in.

Not to mention being naked for the occasion –
So that each rib and muscle shows.
Your left hand already spiked in,
Only the right to wipe the sweat with,

To help yourself to a butt
From the overflowed ashtray,
You won't quite manage to light –
And the night coming, the whiz night.

Charles Simic

Right Dress

Slither of silk like temperate water over
The humps of hips, delicious as a drink;
Lace froths on flesh as lightly as a shadow
And nylon shines, a sly translucent pink.

Next, the sheer stockings smoothing over knees,
Stretched taut at calves and plumping full of thighs.
The curtains at the bedroom windows press
Back, like constables, the straining eyes.

The sweet and private ritual of dressing,
This beautifying of the self, creates
A painless sense of being loved and loving,
A perfect equilibrium of states.

The frock floats like a fall of mist and roses
Over soft secrets, desiring and desired;
Before the wardrobe mirror gravely poses
Archibald Fullblood, Brigadier, retired.

Vernon Scannell

A Blade of Grass

You ask for a poem.
I offer you a blade of grass.
You say it is not good enough.
You ask for a poem.

I say this blade of grass will do.
It has dressed itself in frost,
It is more immediate
Than any image of my making.

You say it is not a poem,
It is a blade of grass and grass
Is not quite good enough.
I offer you a blade of grass.

You are indignant.
You say it is too easy to offer grass.
It is absurd.
Anyone can offer a blade of grass.

You ask for a poem.
And so I write you a tragedy about
How a blade of grass
Becomes more and more difficult to offer,

And about how as you grow older
A blade of grass
Becomes more difficult to accept.

Brian Patten

Alba Einstein

When proof of Einstein's Glaswegian birth
First hit the media everything else was dropped:
Logie Baird, Dundee painters, David Hume - all
Got the big E. Physics documentaries
Became peak-viewing; Scots publishers hurled awa
MacDiarmid like an overbaked potato, and swooped
On the memorabilia: *Einstein Used My Fruitshop,*
Einstein in Old Postcards, Einstein's Bearsden Relatives.
Hot on their heels came the A. E. Fun Park,
Quantum Court, Glen Einstein Highland Malt.
Glasgow was booming. Scotland rose to its feet
At Albert Suppers where The Toast to the General Theory
Was given by footballers, panto-dames, or restauranteurs.
In the US an ageing lab-technician recorded
How the Great Man when excited showed a telltale glottal stop.
He'd loved fiddlers' rallies. His favourite sport was curling.
Thanks to this, Scottish business expanded
Endlessly. His head grew toby-jug-shaped,
Ideal for keyrings. He'd always worn brogues.
Ate bannocks in exile. As a wee boy he'd read *The Beano.*
His name brought new energy: our culture was solidly based
On pride in our hero, The Universal Scot.

Robert Crawford

The Blue Dress

The first November after the divorce
there was a box from my father on my birthday – no card, but a
big box from Hink's, the dark
department store with a balcony and
mahogany rail around the balcony, you could
stand and press your forehead against it
until you could almost feel the dense
grain of the wood, and stare down
into the rows and rows of camisoles,
petticoats, bras, as if looking down
into the lives of women. The box
was from there, he had braved that place for me
the way he had entered my mother once
to get me out. I opened the box – I had
never had a present from him –
and there was a blue shirtwaist dress
blue as the side of a blue teal
disguised to go in safety on the steel-blue water.
I put it on, a perfect fit,
I liked that it was not too sexy, just a
blue dress for a 14-year-old daughter the way
Clark Kent's suit was just a plain suit for a reporter, but I
felt the weave of that mercerised Indian Head cotton
against the skin of my upper arms and my
wide thin back and especially the skin of my
ribs under those new breasts I had
raised in the night like earthworks in commemoration of his name.
A year later, during a fight about
just how awful my father had been,
my mother said he had not picked out the dress,
just told her to get something not too expensive, and then
had not even sent a check for it,
that's the kind of man he was. So I
never wore it again in her sight
but when I went away to boarding school
I wore it all the time there,

loving the feel of it, just
casually mentioning sometimes it was a gift from my father,
wanting in those days to appear to have something
whether it was true or a lie, I didn't care, just to
have something.

Sharon Olds

Busy with Many Jobs

Busy with very urgent jobs
I forgot
one also has
to die

irresponsible
I kept neglecting that duty
or performed it
perfunctorily

as from tomorrow
things will be different

I'll start dying meticulously
wisely optimistically
without wasting time

Tadeusz Różewicz

The Ninth

Aldeburgh Poetry Festival

31 October – 2 November 1997

Revelations

Jean 'Binta' Breeze
Jim Burns
Duncan Bush
Eiléan Ní Chuilleanáin
Jonathan Davidson
Stephen Dobyns
Lavinia Greenlaw
Jaan Kaplinski
Mimi Khalvati
John Kinsella
Liz Lochhead
Les Murray
Ruth Silcock
Anthony Thwaite
Jackie Wills
Glyn Wright

Knowing Plenty

I bought the dish with my pay-off, got the biggest
the roof would hold. There's a lot of domes in Kabul
and different militias. And the tribesmen in New Guinea
wear penis sheaths and rub mud on their bodies,
and the ones in Brazil blow crazy powder up each other's noses,
but if the factions in the eastern suburbs join
with the ones in the south, the Afghan government's
going to have real problems. There's an update due
any minute. But even when shells are falling
you see men carrying cans of water on poles.
And when the Amazon floods it carries away palm trees
and farmers' shacks and dead pigs. And if you stand
in the river having a wee then a tiny fish
will swim deep into your willy and live there,
so don't say I didn't warn you.
Things happen so quickly. I came down from the bathroom
and saw three Afrikaners lying dead in the road.
I went out to let the missus in and diamonds had fallen
two points on Wall Street. You can't afford to be out
for a second. I keep telling her to take her key.
She sits in the kitchen with her head in her arms.
I don't know what's wrong with the woman.
She hasn't been the same since the president
of the World Bank resigned. Or was he sacked? No, that
was the French Foreign Minister over the mess in Africa.
Burundi is about to cut itself to shreds
and the prospects in Guinea are worse than hell,
and the missus keeps wanting to talk about the hole
in the roof where the dish is attached, but I tell her:
As long as you remember to empty the bucket, what's
all the fuss about? And she wants to go to the park.
Park? I said. Park? You've got an equatorial rainforest
coming up after the commercial break, there's a group
of soldiers lost out there. My life. I don't know. Some people.

Then the social called me in, asked what I'd been doing
to find work. Work? I said. Work? The tin miners
in Bolivia have been on strike for a month
and the Chinese silkworm trade has almost collapsed.
He said: But Mr Smith. I said: Don't you try and tell me
about work, one in three Sicilian olive-pickers
has been reduced to begging and the mountain tribes
of Thailand have been forced to grow cabbages. Some people.
Like my missus, she invites her relations round
and they sit here talking. Talking. No interest at all
in the Tokyo banking scandal. She says they don't
understand Japanese. But they never will if they don't
make the effort. I'm learning Croatian from a tape.
I have trouble with their weather forecasters.
They talk so fast, especially when there's shelling
around the TV station. It's been raining since dawn
in Trinidad, and they're expecting a heavy frost
in the eastern parts of Transylvania above a thousand feet.
Oh, and the Mexican president has just been assassinated.
The world's so small nowadays. We know so much.
It's incredible.

Glyn Wright

Living In Real Times

Summer, 1993

In Queen St., Cardiff, I halt to watch in a choice
of screens an over of the Trent Bridge test,
Shane Warne looping wristspin in at
some tailender doomed at best to time-serving

till stumps. Between padded-off balls the eye flickers
to the other channel banked in
other sets, headlines unspooling soundless
beyond Curry's window, the newsreader's mouthings:

a street elsewhere foreshortened
by the long lens. Someone running in the tottering
apologetic way the very frightened run,
as if to panic and sprint could only serve

unfailingly to draw the sniper's bullet. Now
someone whom that bullet has already found. He lies
sprawled amid the usual crazed, cradling women
like one adored at last beyond all dreams.

Sarajevo? Mostar? Vukovar?... TV's intimate and
generalising eye makes everywhere somewhere else:
a province of that small, remote country
of which we, famously, know little

still. While post-modernism makes all things
present, all things post-reality (from the intensity
of this particular and very private grief I realise
I saw these shots two hours ago). Again

the street, down which no doubt the dead man too
had run. Past those same bins, the burned-out
truck, between the building's cover and
a water standpipe. Running partway

then throwing his hands up at it all
and falling dead just at that piece of broken kerb…
As he falls over and over again now in the women's
keening, or in some syndicated twenty-second

filmclip replayed over the next day's news.
Night-time, street, streetlight, a chemist's shop,
wrote Alexander Blok as Russia came apart
(that is, the first time round):

whatever you come to, wherever
you go, it all comes down at last
to this. *You'll die, and just as always start*
the dance again. Over and over. And forever

and for ever. No *Amen.* While from the other end,
on another set, Merv Hughes – that moustache
bigger than Nietzsche's – takes the wicket,
a jubilant slip hurling high the catch, fieldsmen

throwing up their hands, the hangdog batsman
turning away, reluctant as a stood-up groom:
live now, sudden, in real time.
And I wait automatically, lingering

to watch them all do it again, in slowmo,
almost missing it the first time,
trained to the instant replay and the freezeframe:
to the destined fact, knowing there's no way out.

Duncan Bush

Spring Cleaning

de Lord is my shepherd
I shall not want

an she scraping
de las crumbs
aff de plate
knowing ants will feed

maketh me to lie down
in green pastures
leadeth me beside de still
waters

an she han washing clothes
spotless
lifting dem outa de water
drying she han careful slow
pon she apron

restoreth my soul

she mixing
sugar
water
lime
she filling she favourite jug
de one wid de cool palm pattern

yea though I walk
troo de valley of de
shadow of death

she opening de fridge
de cowl stapping her breath
for a motion

I will fear no evil

she put een wah she want
tek out wah she want
shut de door

for thou art wid me
thy rod an thy staff
dey comfort me

an she looking wid a far eye
pon de picture a de children
side a de almanac
pon de wall

surely goodness an mercy
shall follow me

she pick up de broom
an she sweeping

all de days of my life

an she sweeping

an I will dwell
in de house of de Lord

she sweeping out
sweeping
out

shake de broom
in de wind
dus fly
she beat it gains de fence
dus fly
she cup she han
unda de pipe
an she sprinkle water
roun she
stan up
hans akimbo

she watching
all de dark spirits
departing wid de dus

sunrise in er eyes

forever
an ever

Jean 'Binta' Breeze

The Innocence of Radium

With a head full of Swiss clockmakers,
she took a job at a New Jersey factory
painting luminous numbers, copying the style
believed to be found in the candlelit backrooms
of snowbound alpine villages.

Holding each clockface to the light,
she would catch a glimpse of the chemist
as he measured and checked. He was old enough,
had a kind face and a foreign name
she never dared to pronounce: Sochocky.

For a joke she painted her teeth and nails,
jumped out on the other girls walking home.
In bed that night she laughed out loud
and stroked herself with ten green fingertips.
Unable to sleep, the chemist traced each number

on the face he had stolen from the factory floor.
He liked the curve of her eights;
the way she raised the wet brush to her lips
and, with a delicate purse of her mouth,
smoothed the bristle to a perfect tip.

Over the years he watched her grow dull.
The doctors gave up, removed half her jaw,
and blamed syphilis when her thighbone snapped
as she struggled up a flight of steps.
Diagnosing infidelity, the chemist pronounced

the innocence of radium, a kind of radiance
that could not be held by the body of a woman,
only caught between her teeth. He was proud
of his paint and made public speeches
on how it could be used by artists to convey

the quality of moonlight. Sochocky displayed
these shining landscapes on his walls;
his faith sustained alone in a room
full of warm skies that broke up the dark
and drained his blood of its colour.

His dangerous bones could not keep their secret.
Laid out for X-ray, before a single button was pressed,
they exposed the plate and pictured themselves
as a ghost, not a skeleton, a photograph
he was unable to stop being developed and fixed.

Lavinia Greenlaw

The Elocution Lesson

'Feel me breathe, girls,' –
Miss Bannerman places
Our pink open hands
On her emerald dress.

She presses our palms
Across thick, crinkly wool,
Our fingers extend
Along muscles and ribs.

'In – Out, In – Out,'
Miss Bannerman breathes,
Her bony chest heaves,
In – Out go our hands.

Our hands are pink fans
That Miss Bannerman breathes
Into movement, *In – Out*,
By the strength of her ribs.

Miss Bannerman's hair
Is a bright wavy brown,
Her lips are bright red,
Her body bright green,

Her eyes dark and sad,
Her thin ribs alive –
One by one, we draw back
While Miss Bannerman breathes.

Ruth Silcock

Cockroach Story

'The reason for a cockroach in a story must differ from the reason for a cockroach in a kitchen.'

Leon Wieseltier, TLS

It was not home. It was in Tokyo
At half-past ten at night or thereabouts.
I went into the kitchen, flicked the switch,
And saw him crouching on the table's edge.

He was enormous, brown, and very still.
His feathery branches waited, so it seemed,
For further movement, and for me to move.
We looked at one another very hard.

He did not move, nor did I, watching him.
The jet-lag left me drowsy still, though sleep
Seemed far away, as I was far away.
I studied him as if in Japanese.

Aburamushi is the name for him
I suddenly remembered, wondering
What *abura* means: *mushi* is 'insect' or
A dozen other things in Japanese,

Such as a kind of soup, both clear and poached.
This cockroach, though, was more a samurai,
Plated and helmeted and plumed and proud.
I faced him as a common yokel might,

Lest he should shove me sideways with his sword,
Or leap across the tabletop and land
Bristling with fury in my sweating hair.
It was a hot September night, and I

Was tired of travel. 'I'll get it over with –
This stinker from the floorboards makes me sick,'
I thought, 'and I am sick of fantasy.'
I took one slipper off and lunged at him.

He skidded off the table, hit the floor
With a soft slushy plop, and sidestepped back
Towards the sink. I threw myself full-length
And smashed him with the slipper, and crouched down.

His scales fanned out. He bled onto the boards,
Gave half a shrug, and then lay still and dead.
I wiped the slipper with a newspaper,
Rinsed both my hands, and groped my way to bed.

That is the story. This is the poem, told
In metre, with a rhyme to end it all,
The reasons for the cockroach, or the poem,
Or why I've told the story – who can tell?

A cockroach in a kitchen is the truth.
A cockroach in a story may be lies.
The insect was both noble and uncouth.
The writer makes a life from mysteries.

Anthony Thwaite

A Manager Writes

Except for the second half, last week's game
was our best game, not counting that game

against Bury. I thought we shouldn't have lost,
but even though we did all is not lost,

there's still today and we've got everything
to play for. Life can be a funny thing

and I know I am not alone in saying
good luck lads for today's game. In saying

good luck lads what I really mean to say
is they won't need it 'cause they're the best, but say

we went two nil down in the first minute,
and I think I'm right in saying a minute

is all it takes sometimes to score a goal,
or two – I remember that fourth goal

we conceded against Burnley, I'd say,
and I think Managers should have their say,

that that goal was a quick goal, and it's goals
we need, as long as the goals are our goals.

Before I sign off I'd like to say thanks
to Brian Jones of the Supporters' Club. Thanks,

Brian. You certainly saved the day on Saturday.
Let's hope it doesn't happen again this Saturday.

Having said that I'd just like to agree
with what I said last week. We all agree

here at the Club that winning is our aim,
football's our game, and I for one will aim

to win, although of course I'm not playing
but for those who are playing, it's the playing

that's important, as long as we win as well.

Jonathan Davidson

Counting

Susan wants to attach scythes to the wheels
of her father's car and cut everyone off at the knees,
like Boadicea. She could flatten a town centre
as quickly as a combine harvester. She's referee
when I fight with Donna over a ruler, snapped,
beating a cage of locusts so they would try to escape.
As we smash each other against lockers, Susan counts.

Every thud on metal is a point. Outside the art room
she throttles me for losing and my throat stings with vomit
as an undigested pea is forced from my nostril.
When I jump on her head in the swimming pool
her gushing nose leaves a trail on the white tiles like steak
dripping inside our fridge. But we make peace in needlework,
sewing skirts short enough to be cut from remnants.

They will flap against our buttocks like shirt-tails
when we meet on Saturday in the Army and Navy café,
wrists smudged with lipstick – Fuchsia, Pink Passion,
Carnival, Hot Date. We put them on in the toilet mirror,
practising open-mouthed kisses on folded tissues –
the fine lines of our lips printed like the claws
of hungry birds treading lightly over snow.

Jackie Wills

The Silo

Visitors, as if they knew, never remarked
on the old silo with its rammed earth walls
and high thatched roof, incongruous amongst
the new machinery and silver field bins.
Nor the workers brought in at harvest time,
trucks rolling past the ghostly whimperings,
snarls and sharp howls cutting the thick silo's
baffling. Nor when a bumper harvest filled
every bin and the farmer was hungry
for space – no-one ever mentioned bringing
the old silo back into service. This
had been the way for as far back as could
be remembered. Thin sprays of baby's breath
grew around its foundations, while wedding
bouquet sprouted bizarrely from the grey
mat of thatching. The sun had bleached the walls
bone-white while the path to the heavily
bolted door was of red earth, a long thin
stream of unhealthy blood. Before those storms
which brew thickly on summer evenings
red-tailed black cockatoos settled in waves,
sparking the straw like a volcano, dark
fire erupting from the heart of the white
silo, trembling with energy deeper
than any anchorage earth could offer.
And lightning dragging a moon's bleak halo
to dampen the eruption, with thunder
echoing out over the bare paddocks
towards the farmhouse where an old farmer
consoled his bitter wife on the fly-proof
verandah, cursing the cockatoos, hands
describing a prison from which neither
could hope for parole, petition, release.

John Kinsella

Walking with my Father

Walking with my father
we'd go to parts of the town
I didn't know. He'd direct
strangers to destinations
I thought mysterious,
and he'd take me to shops
with shelves of things
I found exotic.

Walking with my father,
I'd hear him say that most crooks
weren't in prison,
they were in business,
and I'd be told
never to jangle coins in my pocket
in case a poor man heard them
and felt he was being taunted.

Walking with my father,
I learnt more about the world
than any schoolteacher taught me,
though my father also told me
to listen to what a teacher said,
to keep my mouth shut and ears open,
and to always use my eyes
for what they were intended.

Walking with my father,
I knew how he had walked this way
with his father,
and how the words were passed on.
I knew my grandfather,
and all those who were before him.
I walked through history,
and knew where it came from.

Jim Burns

from: Entries on Light

I love all things in miniature
	– the blue tree whose sprigs
are like the lilac's in miniature –
	and small things too since they
recollect a child's eye view
	of a small world inside a large
in which small things might represent
	the large – acorn cup a cup, sprig
a tree – and because miniatures are
	fully-formed and in completion
futureless, as if childhood itself
	were arrested, made redeemable.

Lying belly down on grass, level
	with a sparrow's eye as it cocks
its head, engages without seeing us
	I remember how our first lessons
were tailored to a scale in which
	the child loomed large, creatures
small and therefore it was incumbent
	on our stature to feel tenderness.
I felt it for a moment and have lost it
	now that the mind has taken flight
left a birdless stretch of grass
	so much larger than itself.

Mimi Khalvati

How To Like It

These are the first days of fall. The wind
at evening smells of roads still to be travelled,
while the sound of leaves blowing across the lawns
is like an unsettled feeling in the blood,
the desire to get in a car and just keep driving.
A man and a dog descend their front steps.
The dog says, Let's go downtown and get crazy drunk.
Let's tip over all the trash cans we can find.
This is how dogs deal with the prospect of change.
But in his sense of the season, the man is struck
by the oppressiveness of his past, how his memories
which were shifting and fluid have grown more solid
until it seems he can see remembered faces
caught up among the dark places in the trees.
The dog says, Let's pick up some girls and just
rip off their clothes. Let's dig holes everywhere.
Above his house, the man notices wisps of cloud
crossing the face of the moon. Like in a movie,
he says to himself, a movie about a person
leaving on a journey. He looks down the street
to the hills outside of town and finds the cut
where the road heads north. He thinks of driving
on that road and the dusty smell of the car
heater, which hasn't been used since last winter.
The dog says, Let's go down to the diner and sniff
people's legs. Let's stuff ourselves on burgers.
In the man's mind, the road is empty and dark.
Pine trees press down to the edge of the shoulder,
where the eyes of animals, fixed in his headlights,
shine like small cautions against the night.
Sometimes a passing truck makes his whole car shake.
The dog says, Let's go to sleep. Let's lie down
by the fire and put our tails over our noses.
But the man wants to drive all night, crossing
one state line after another, and never stop
until the sun creeps into his rearview mirror.

Then he'll pull over and rest awhile before
starting again, and at dusk he'll crest a hill
and there, filling a valley, will be the lights
of a city entirely new to him.
But the dog says, Let's just go back inside.
Let's not do anything tonight. So they
walk back up the sidewalk to the front steps.
How is it possible to want so many things
and still want nothing? The man wants to sleep
and wants to hit his head again and again
against a wall. Why is it all so difficult?
But the dog says, Let's go make a sandwich.
Let's make the tallest sandwich anyone's ever seen.
And that's what they do and that's where the man's
wife finds him, staring into the refrigerator
as if into the place where the answers are kept –
the ones telling why you get up in the morning
and how it is possible to sleep at night,
answers to what comes next and how to like it.

Stephen Dobyns

Kidspoem/Bairnsang

It wis January
and a gey dreich day
the first day I went to the school
so
ma Mum happed me up in ma good navyblue nap coat
wi the rid tartan hood
birled a scarf aroon ma neck
pu'ed on ma pixie and ma pawkies
it wis that bitter
said
'noo ye'll no starve'
gied me a wee kiss and a kidoan skelp on the bum
and sent me off across the playground
to the place I'd learn to say
'It was January
and a really dismal day
the first day I went to school
so
my Mother wrapped me up in my best navyblue top coat
with the red tartan hood
twirled a scarf around my neck
pulled on my bobble-hat and mittens
it was so bitterly cold
said
"now you won't freeze to death"
gave me a little kiss and a pretend slap on the bottom
and sent me off across the playground
to the place I'd learn to forget to say
"It wis January
and a gey dreich day
the first day I went to the school
so
ma Mum happed me up in ma good navyblue nap coat
wi the rid tartan hood
birled a scarf aroon ma neck
pu'ed on ma pixie and ma pawkies
it was that bitter."'

Oh,
saying it was one thing
but when it came to writing it
in black and white
the way it had to be said
was as if
you were grown up, posh, male, English and dead.

Liz Lochhead

That Summer

So what did she do that summer
When they were all out working?

If she moved she felt a soft rattle
That settled like a purseful of small change.
She staggered through the quiet of the house,
Leaned on a flowering doorpost
And went back inside from the glare
Feeling in her skirt pocket the skin on her hands,
Never so smooth since her fourteenth year.

One warm evening they were late;
She walked across the yard with a can,
Watered a geranium and kept on going
Till she came to the ridge looking over the valley
At the low stacked hills, the steep ground
Between that plunged like a funnel of sand.
She couldn't face back home, they came for her
As she stood watching the hills breathing out and in,
Their dialogue of hither and yon.

Eiléan Ní Chuilleanáin

'Death does not come from outside'

Death does not come from outside. Death is within.
Born-grows together with us.
Goes with us to kindergarten and school.
Learns with us to read and count.
Goes sledging with us, and to the pictures.
Seeks with us the meaning of life.
Tries to make sense with us of Einstein and Wiener.
Makes with us our first sexual contacts.
Marries, bears children, quarrels, makes up.
Separates, or perhaps not, with us.
Goes to work, goes to the doctor, goes camping,
to the convalescent home and the sanatorium. Grows old,
sees children married, retired,
looks after grandchildren, grows ill, dies
with us. Let us not fear, then. Our death
will not outlive us.

Jaan Kaplinski

It Allows a Portrait in Line Scan at Fifteen

He retains a slight 'Martian' accent, from the years of single phrases.
He no longer hugs to disarm. It is gradually allowing him affection.
It does not allow proportion. Distress is absolute, shrieking, and runs him at frantic speed through crashing doors.
He likes cyborgs. Their taciturn power, with his intonation.
It still runs him around the house, alone in the dark, cooing and laughing.
He can read about soils, populations and New Zealand. On neutral topics he's illiterate.
Arnie Schwarzenegger is an actor. He isn't a cyborg really, is he, Dad?
He lives on forty acres, with animals and trees, and used to draw it continually.
He knows the map of Earth's fertile soils, and can draw it freehand.
He can only lie in a panicked shout *SorrySorryIdidn'tdoit!* warding off conflict with others and himself.
When he ran away constantly it was to the greengrocers to worship stacked fruit.
His favourite country was the Ukraine: it is nearly all deep fertile soil.
Giggling, he climbed all over the dim Freudian psychiatrist who told us how autism resulted from 'refrigerator' parents.
When asked to smile, he photographs a rictus-smile on his face.
It long forbade all naturalistic films. They were Adult movies.
If they (that is, he) *are bad the police will put them in hospital.*
He sometimes drew the farm amid Chinese or Balinese rice terraces.
When a runaway, he made uproar in the police station, playing at three times adult speed.
Only animated films were proper. *Who Framed Roger Rabbit* then authorised the rest.
Phrases spoken to him he would take as teaching, and repeat.
When he worshipped fruit, he screamed as if poisoned when it was fed to him.
A one-word first conversation: *Blane. – Yes! Plane, that's right, baby! – Blane.*
He has forgotten nothing, and remembers the precise quality of experiences.
It requires rulings: *Is stealing very playing up, as bad as murder?*
He counts at a glance, not looking. And he has never been lost.

When he ate only nuts and dried fruit, words were for dire emergencies.
He knows all the breeds of fowls, and the counties of Ireland.
He'd begun to talk, then returned to babble, then silence. It withdrew
speech for years.
Is that very autistic, to play video games in the day?
He is anger's mirror, and magnifies any near him, raging it down.
It still won't allow him fresh fruit, or orange juice with bits in it.
He swam in the midwinter dam at night. It had no rules about cold.
He was terrified of thunder and finally cried as if in explanation *It – angry!*
He grilled an egg he'd broken into bread. Exchanges of soil-knowledge
are called landtalking.
He lives in objectivity. I was sure Bell's palsy would leave my face only
when he said it had begun to.
Don't say word! when he was eight forbade the word 'autistic' in his
presence.
Bantering questions about girlfriends cause a terrified look and blocked
ears.
He sometimes centred the farm in a furrowed American midwest.
Eye contact, Mum! means he truly wants attention. It dislikes I-contact.
He is equitable and kind, and only ever a little jealous. It was a relief
when that little arrived.
He surfs, bowls, walks for miles. For many years he hasn't trailed his
left arm while running.
I gotta get smart! looking terrified into the years. *I gotta get smart!*

Les Murray

The Tenth

Aldeburgh Poetry Festival

6 – 8 November 1998

Celebration

Dannie Abse
Simon Armitage
Allan E. Baker
Kevin Crossley-Holland
Kwame Dawes
Helen Dunmore
Sophie Hannah
Rita Ann Higgins
M. C. Jabber
Kathleen Jamie
August Kleinzahler
Christopher Logue
John Lynch
Jamie McKendrick
Olive Senior
Jean Sprackland
Shuntarō Tanikawa
Frances Wilson

Some Tentative Definitions I

"*Lickle more drums...*"
Bob Marley

First the snare crack,
a tight-head snare crack like steel,
rattle, then cut, snap,
crack sharp and ring at the tail;
calling in a mellow mood,
with the bass, a looping lanky
dread, sloping like a lean-to,
defying gravity and still limping
to a natural half-beat riddim,
on this rain-slick avenue.

Sounds come in waves
like giddy party types
bringing their own style and fashion,
their own stout and rum,
their own Irish Moss
to this ram jam session.

Everything get like water now
the way steady hands
curve round a sweat-smooth waistline,
guiding the rub, the dub, so ready.
This sound is Rock Steady
syrup slow melancholy,
the way the guitar tickling
a bedrock drum and bass,
shimmering light over miry clay.

Kwame Dawes

St. Bride's

So this is women's work: folding
and unfolding, be it linen or a selkie-
skin tucked behind a rock. Consider

the hare in jizzen: her leverets' ears
flat as the mizzen of a ship
entering a bottle. A thread's trick;

adders uncoil into Spring. Feathers
of sunlight, glanced from a butterknife
quiver on the ceiling,

and a last sharp twist for the shoulders
delivers my daughter, the placenta
following, like a fist of purple kelp.

Kathleen Jamie

The Shout

We went out
into the school yard together, me and the boy
whose name and face

I don't remember. We were testing the range
of the human voice:
he had to shout for all he was worth,

I had to raise an arm
from across the divide to signal back
that the sound had carried.

He called from over the park – I lifted an arm.
Out of bounds,
he yelled from the end of the road,

from the foot of the hill,
from beyond the look-out post of Fretwell's Farm –
I lifted an arm.

He left town, went on to be twenty years dead
with a gunshot hole
in the roof of his mouth, in Western Australia.

Boy with the name and face I don't remember,
you can stop shouting now, I can still hear you.

Simon Armitage

The Marble Fly

The guide crinkled his nose
like a squirrel with a nut
as he pointed out to us
the baked-clay phallus
on the oven door, no doubt
symbolic of the risen loaf.

Red dust and stone thresholds
to an unrecovered world,
stone fruit that Felix
the fruitseller sold, stone-cold
drinks from the hot drinks stall,
wheel ruts cut in the stone road.

Murals, mosaics, mysteries:
the pierced stag, the girl's back
exposed to the beaded whip,
a lion mauling the shift of Thisbe
whilst a wall-eyed Pyramus
has severed an artery.

A wall relief in the Wool Market
shows the animal world in marble
– a lizard canopening a cricket,
a mouse airlifted by an owl
and a fly (watch out, fly!)
on its own among the bulrushes –

all perfectly preserved and just
a shade larger than lifesize
and much stiller than life and harder.
It can't have been long after
that much the same idea
occurred to Vesuvius.

Jamie McKendrick

Three Ways of Recovering a Body

By chance I was alone in my bed the morning
I woke to find my body had gone.
It had been coming. I'd cut off my hair in sections
so each of you would have something to remember,
then my nails worked loose from their beds
of oystery flesh. Who was it got them?
One night I slipped out of my skin. It lolloped
hooked to my heels, hurting. I had to spray on
more scent so you could find me in the dark,
I was going so fast. One of you begged for my ears
because you could hear the sea in them.

First I planned to steal myself back. I was a mist
on thighs, belly and hips. I'd slept with so many men.
I was with you in the ash-haunted stations of Poland,
I was with you on that grey plaza in Berlin
while you wolfed three doughnuts without stopping,
thinking yourself alone. Soon I recovered my lips
by waiting behind the mirror while you shaved.
You pouted. I peeled away kisses like wax
no longer warm to the touch. Then I flew off.

Next I decided to become a virgin. Without a body
it was easy to make up a new story. In seven years
every invisible cell would be renewed
and none of them would have touched any of you.
I went to a cold lake, to a grey-lichened island,
I was gold in the wallet of the water.
I was known to the inhabitants, who were in love
with the coveted whisper of my virginity:
all too soon they were bringing me coffee and perfume,
cash under stones. I could really do something for them.

Thirdly I tried marriage to a good husband
who knew my past but forgave it. I believed in the power
of his penis to smoke out all those men
so that bit by bit my body service would resume,
although for a while I'd be the one woman in the world
who was only present in the smile of her vagina.
He stroked the air where I might have been.
I turned to the mirror and saw mist gather
as if someone lived in the glass. Recovering
I breathed to myself '*Hold on! I'm coming.*'

Helen Dunmore

from: New Numbers

'I need a drink

I mean, I have been drinking.

I mean that I am drunk.'

'Oh come...'

'I mean I am a drunkard.
Drunk. An alcoholic. Drunk.
Look in my bag. Vodka. No ice.
I have been drunk since I got up.'

Tomatoes on toast in the still of the night
reading Milton.
You have grown old. 'That old guy with the book.'
You heard it in a queue and felt afraid.

'... for god's sake leave me *alone*.
I am weak. I have lost my looks.
I cannot get on with myself.
Day after day I stare at the oven.'

Dogs howl beneath high windows
and the cries of people being tortured fill the air
and the cries of their torturers drown them out
but they cry even louder
and their torturers go mad with frustration

and the girl who read your hand
in that milk bar in Wrexham,
what happened to *her*?

Will my work help you hoe your row?
Are mine good books to have
when you are ill in bed in a foreign country?

Christopher Logue

THE CREATION

In the beginning God made the world
out of a No. 83 Meccano Set
which is the biggest Meccano Set
in all the world
which God made out of it
and which is Model No. 46.

Then God made Adam, who is Model No. 98,
in his own likeness
and Adam saw the world and it was good
and Adam said to God
'Who made this world? For it is good.'
And God said to Adam
'It was I who made it
out of a No. 83 Meccano Set.'
And Adam said to God
'Who made the No. 83 Meccano Set?'
And God said to Adam
'Meccano Ltd.
Binns Road
Liverpool 13.'
And Adam gave great thanks to God and said
'But, Lord, I am alone.'

And God said
'Let there be Hornby Trains.'
And there were Hornby Trains.

A. E. Baker

Deadnettle

Sprawled under the hedge he snaps
the thin necks of deadnettle,
pinches the white sac, squirts
nectar into my mouth.
A small sweet promise on the tongue.

I run home in the heat. The smell
of melting tar, a stickiness underfoot.
The house whirrs and stutters with the machine.
She urges a small red dress to the needle.

She stops, examines me, stretches
to tug a snag of stickybud from my hair.
'Be a good girl.' She takes up the cloth

and snaps the thread on her teeth. 'Won't you?'

Jean Sprackland

Changes

There was a time when we were just a pair of heads:
the one that hung above her cot like a frozen moon,
and the one that sang
while she suckled into heaven.

But before we knew it, our heads had grown stilts:
escapees from The War of the Worlds
on scraps of paper
Blu-tacked to the wall.

Now, we have hands with knife fingers;
we have penguin feet, pumpkin faces,
and the sun is an orange spider
in the top right hand corner of the sky.

Masterpieces in the cupboard under the stairs,
we treasure these days of black crayon;
the free sweep of a thick brush;
a time of infinite simile.

Soon, she'll leave us at the school gate
for a world of ruler, rubber and compass;
where things must look only like themselves,
and we'll wonder what will become of us.

John Lynch

Revisiting the Pigs

Once you've checked the nails you hammered
last summer into the oak are holding,
and the sparrow's skull and bits of candle
are safely hidden, you slope off to see
if the pigs are still there. And they are,
doing all the things pigs are supposed to do –

snuffling and grunting and wallowing in mud
like log-jams, then heaving their overweight up
as if they'll never make it, to sit for a moment
amazed to be upright, before lumbering over
to look at you sidelong, whiskery, curious,
snouts like soft buttons, tails coming undone.

Surprise, reassurance, relief, that they
go on doing all this – as if you might find
last summer's best friend from next door
still wants to play the same games, isn't
wearing mascara, a sweater you'd be forbidden,
isn't ever so sorry, but she's just going out.

Frances Wilson

Translation Workshop: Grit and Blood

Hige sceal pe heardra, heorte pe cenre,
mod sceal pe mare, pe ure maegen lytlad!
Word-stand, locking shield-wall
not to be broken down, nor even
translated in its own bright coin.
Courage, intention, resolve – won't do.
Out with Latinates! I want earth-words,
tough roots: grit and blood, grunt, gleam.

Harder heads and hearts more keen,
spirits on fire as our strength flags!
Here lies our leader, axed and limp,
the top dog in the dust. He who turns
from this war-play now will mourn
for ever. I am old. I'll stay put.
I'll lay my pillow on the ground
beside my dear man, my loved lord.

Kevin Crossley-Holland

The Did-You-Come-Yets of the Western World

When he says to you:
You look so beautiful
you smell so nice –
how I've missed you –
and did you come yet?

It means nothing,
and he is smaller
than a mouse's fart.

Don't listen to him...
Go to Annaghdown Pier
with your father's rod.
Don't necessarily hold out
for the biggest one;
oftentimes the biggest ones
are the smallest in the end.

Bring them all home,
but not together.
One by one is the trick;
avoid red herrings and scandal.

Maybe you could take two
on the shortest day of the year.
Time is the cheater here
not you, so don't worry.

Many will bite the usual bait;
they will talk their slippery way
through fine clothes and expensive perfume,
fishing up your independence.

These are
the did-you-come-yets of the western world,
the feather and fin rufflers.
Pity for them they have no wisdom.

Others will bite at any bait.
Maggot, suspender, or dead worm.
Throw them to the sharks.

In time one will crawl
out from under thigh-land.
Although drowning he will say,

'Woman I am terrified, why is this house
shaking?'

And you'll know he's the one.

Rita Ann Higgins

An Interrupted Letter

In this room's winterlight the travail of
a letter to a new widow. Solemn,
the increasing enterprise of age.
I stutter. Consoling words come slow,
seem false, as if spoken on a stage.
It would be easier to send flowers.

I think of her closing her husband's eyelids
and I look up. Siberian snow hesitated,
then parachuted into our garden
for hours, confiscating yesterday's
footprints. Shall I send flowers?

But now my wife, unaware in the far kitchen,
suddenly sings, captivating me,
my pen mid-air above a muffled page.

When we were young, tremulant with Spring,
often off-key she'd sing her repertoire –
dateless folk songs, dance tunes dated.
In her Pears-suds bath I'd hear her,
in the Morris Minor with our kids.

I must return to my hiemal letter.
Sing on love, as once you did, sing and sing
for past youth, for hungers unabated.

Dannie Abse

Ticket to Staines

I'd emerged from the second of two freezing trains
With a bag full of cheese salad sandwich remains
When I met a tree surgeon who said he was broke
And asked me to buy him a ticket to Staines.

He told me a jumbled, unfortunate tale
About how he had broken the terms of his bail
And he had to get back to his Mum's before ten
Or the cops would be taking him straight back to jail.

He told me his story outside Euston station
Describing his crime and its justification:
His tree surgeon's chainsaw had sliced through a train
In an effort to sabotage veal transportation.

His Mum had lumbago and no credit card
For a telephone booking. I thought long and hard
And it seemed to be me and me only that stood
Between him and a grilling at New Scotland Yard.

With diminishing faith in the state of my brains
And without quite condoning the slicing of trains
I led him past Knickerbox, Sock Shop and all
And bought that tree surgeon a ticket to Staines.

What will become of him? Where will he go?
(And don't say, 'You paid for it, you ought to know.')
I mean, is there a place for him? Is there a place
For a lawbreaking tree surgeon, chainsaw in tow?

There's a place for the tyrant who rules and constrains,
For the person who keeps other people in chains.
Wherever that tree surgeon goes, freedom reigns.
I wish I could see him arriving in Staines.

Sophie Hannah

from: Project

Bodies unfurling, hurling, swirling out of sight.
Slide finger under flap and move from left to right.
To open, pinch the sides of the carton tightly.
Apply *Swarfega* with a forefinger nightly.
If symptoms persist, consult your local GP.
Look into my eyes, are you feeling sleepy?
Let the words hypnotise, it's so creepy
The way they can take up residence so deeply
Inside the centre of your mind, then just as quickly
Fa-*ay-ay*-de away - are you still with me?
Or did you lose me some time earlier this evening?
Like Brian Keenan, John McCarthy, you're beginning
To feel what it's like to be free, no longer a hostage.
There's 30% vegetable fat in this sausage.
Warning: Accidents prohibited on this road.
Don't forget to use your fucking postcode.
Excuse me, sir, are you the owner of this vehicle?
It's not that I don't trust you. I just need empirical
Evidence to form a verifiable deduction.
No animals were hurt during the making of this production.
Any resemblance to actual persons living or dead
Is entirely coincidental day our daily bread
And forgive us our trespasses as we forgive those
Who trespass against us - I'll outlive those
Who think they are gangsters just cos they can say 'yo'
El muy gran y grosso oleoso
Défense de fumer, é periculoso,
As *Cypress Hill* said, don't ya know I'm going loco!
Ell-oh-see-oh, let's do the locomotion.
Do not use while the train is in motion.
Please deposit in the receptacle provided.
I'll be whatever you want, cos I've decided
That what I am, who I am is your decision.
The management reserves the right to refuse admission.
I'm putting it topical, ultimately disposable,
Take me and throw me away as soon as possible.
Warning: contents may settle in transit.

If you were telepathic, I'd start thinking in Sanskrit.
Excuse me, could you tell me where the nearest church is?
Please consume within three days of purchase.
I feel the need to kneel and ask forgiveness.
Due to insolvency, we're closed for business.

M. C. Jabber

Watching Young Couples with an Old Girlfriend on Sunday Morning

How mild these young men seem to me now
with their baggy shorts and clouds of musk,
as if younger brothers of the women they escort
in tight black leather, bangs and tattoos,
cute little toughies, so Louise Brooks annealed

in MTV, headed off for huevos rancheros
and the Sunday *Times* at some chic, crowded dive.
I don't recall it at all this way, do you?
How sweetly complected and confident they look,
their faces unclouded by the rages

and abandoned, tearful couplings of the night before,
the drunkenness, beast savor and remorse.
Or do I recoil from their youthfulness and health?
Oh, not recoil, just fail to see ourselves.
And yet, this tenderness between us that remains

was mortared first with a darkness that got loose, a frenzy,
we still, we still refuse to name.

August Kleinzahler

Hurricane Story, 1988

My mother wasn't christened
Imelda but she stashed a cache
of shoes beneath the bed.

She used to travel to Haiti,
Panama, Curacao, Miami,
wherever there was bargain

to catch – even shoes that
didn't have match. Back home
she could always find customer

come bend-down to look and talk
where she plant herself on
sidewalk. When the hurricane

hit, she ban her belly and bawl,
for five flights a day to Miami
grounded. No sale and her shoes

getting junjo from the damp (since
the roof decamp) and the rest
sitting in Customs, impounded.

My mother banked between her
breasts, lived out her dreams
in a spliff or two each night.

Since the storm, things so tight
her breasts shrivel, the notes
shrinking. Every night she there

thinking. Every morning she get up
and she wail: Lawd! Life so soak-up
and no bail out. To raatid!

Olive Senior

Evening

When I got home in the evening
Dad was dead on the doorstep.
    'Strange things happen', I thought,
stepped over him and went inside to find
Mom dead in the kitchen.
The gas range was still burning.
I turned it off and tasted the stew.
    'Well, if things keep going like this
my older brother must be dead, too.'
Sure enough, he was dead in the tub.
The kid next door made believe he was crying.
The noodle vendor's bike brakes were screeching.
It was an ordinary evening,
promising no relief tomorrow.

Shuntarō Tanikawa

Acknowledgements

For permission to reprint copyright material, the publishers gratefully acknowledge the following:

Dannie Abse and Hutchinson Press for 'An Interrupted Letter' from *Arcadia, One Mile* (1998).
Fleur Adcock and Oxford University Press for 'Against Coupling' from *Selected Poems* (1983).
John Agard and Serpent's Tail for 'Palm Tree King' from *Mangoes and Bullets* (1990).
Moniza Alvi and Bloodaxe Books for 'Indian Cooking' from *Carrying My Wife* (2000).
Simon Armitage for 'The Shout'.
Donald Atkinson and Peterloo Poets for 'Wailing Begins at the House-Wall' from *A Sleep of Drowned Fathers* (1989).
Allan E. Baker for 'The Creation' from *Smiths Knoll 15*.
Sebastian Barker and Enitharmon Press for an extract from 'Advertisement for Itself' from *Guarding the Border* (1992).
Patricia Beer's Estate and Carcanet Press for 'In a Country Museum' from *Collected Poems* (1988).
Connie Bensley and Bloodaxe Books for 'A Friendship' from *Central Reservations* (1990).
Judi Benson and Rockingham Press for 'Says the Southerner' from *In the Pockets of Strangers* (1993).
Anne Beresford and Marion Boyars for 'Love Song of the Thracian Horseman' from *Songs a Thracian Taught Me* (1980).
James Berry and New Beacon Books for 'From Lucy: A Favour' from *Lucy's Letters and Loving* (1982).
Sujata Bhatt and Carcanet Press for 'Love in a Bathtub' from *Point No Point* (1997).
Peter Bland and Carcanet Press for 'Two Family Snaps' from *Selected Poems* (1987).
Charles Boyle and Carcanet Press for 'Crawley Welcomes Careful Drivers' from *The Very Man* (1993).
Jean 'Binta' Breeze and Virago Press for 'Spring Cleaning' from *Spring Cleaning* (1992).
Alan Brownjohn and Hutchinson Press for 'The Automatic Days' from *The Observation Car* (1990).
Jim Burns and Redbeck Press for 'Walking With My Father' from *Confessions of an Old Believer* (1996).

John Burnside and Cape Poetry for 'The Myth of the Twin' from *The Myth of the Twin* (1994).
Duncan Bush and Seren for 'Living in Real Times' from *Masks* (1994).
Liz Cashdan for 'Cutting Loose' from *New Women Poets* (Bloodaxe Books 1990).
Nina Cassian and Forest Books for 'Temptation' from *Call Yourself Alive?* translated by Andrea Deletant & Brenda Walker (1988).
Charles Causley and Macmillan Publishers for 'Eden Rock' from *A Field of Vision* (1988).
Eiléan Ní Chuilleanáin and The Gallery Press for 'That Summer' from *The Brazen Serpent* (1994).
Gillian Clarke and Carcanet Press for 'Neighbours' from *Letting in the Rumour* (1989).
David Constantine and Bloodaxe Books for 'Eldon Hole' from *Madder* (1987).
Wendy Cope and Faber & Faber for 'Names' from *Serious Concerns* (1992).
Robert Crawford and Chatto & Windus for 'Alba Einstein' from *A Scottish Assembly* (1990).
Iain Crichton Smith's Estate and Carcanet Press for 'That Island Formed You' from *Selected Poems* (1981).
Kevin Crossley-Holland and Enitharmon Press for 'Translation Workshop: Grit and Blood' from *The Language of Yes* (1996).
Duncan Curry and Smith/Doorstop Books for 'The Bottom Back Nut' from *The Darts and the Commentary* (1996).
Tony Curtis and Poetry Wales Press for 'Soup' from *Selected Poems* (1986).
Adam Czerniawski and Bloodaxe Books for 'Fish' from *The Burning Forest* translated by the author (1988).
David Dabydeen and Dangaroo Press for 'Catching Crabs' from *Coolie Odyssey* (1988).
Jonathan Davidson and Arc Publications for 'A Manager Writes' from *The Living Room* (1994).
Kwame Dawes and Peepal Tree Press for 'Some Tentative Definitions I' from *Shook Foil* (1997).
Nuala Ní Dhomhnaill and The Gallery Press for 'The Language Issue' translated by Paul Muldoon from *Pharaoh's Daughter* (1990).
Stephen Dobyns and Bloodaxe Books for 'How to Like It' from *Velocities* (1996).
Maura Dooley and Bloodaxe Books for 'Apple Pie in Pizzaland' from *Explaining Magnetism* (1991).

Carol Ann Duffy and Anvil Press Poetry for 'Translating the English, 1989' from *The Other Country* (1990).
Ian Duhig and Bloodaxe Books for 'From The Irish' from *The Bradford Count* (1991).
Helen Dunmore and Bloodaxe Books for 'Three Ways of Recovering a Body' from *Recovering a Body* (1994).
Douglas Dunn and Faber & Faber for 'Reading Pascal in the Lowlands' from *Selected Poems 1964 - 1983* (1986).
Jane Duran and Enitharmon Press for 'Braided Rug' from *Breathe Now, Breathe* (1995).
Lauris Edmond and Bloodaxe Books for 'Hymns Ancient and Modern' from *New and Selected Poems* (1992).
Robert Etty and Slow Dancer Press for 'Some Notes About a Hare' from *Marking Places* (1994).
Vicki Feaver and Cape Poetry for 'Lily Pond' from *The Handless Maiden* (1994).
James Fenton and King Penguin for 'The Skip' from *The Memory of War and Children in Exile* (1983).
Peter Finch and Seren for 'The Tattoo' from *Selected Poems* (1987).
Janet Fisher and Smith/Doorstop Books for 'Fifty Years On' from *Listening to Dancing* (1996).
Duncan Forbes and Enitharmon Press for 'The Stars' from *Public & Confidential* (1989).
John Fuller and Chatto & Windus for 'Wednesday' from *The Grey Among The Green* (1988).
Judy Gahagan and Flambard Press for 'Mourning' from *Crossing the No-man's Land* (1999).
Dana Gioia and Peterloo Poets for 'Planting a Sequoia' from *The Gods of Winter* (1991).
Mick Gowar and Viking Kestrel, Penguin Books for 'Scary Monsters' from *Third Time Lucky* (1988).
Lavinia Greenlaw and Faber & Faber for 'The Innocence of Radium' from *Night Photograph* (1993).
Andrew Greig and Bloodaxe Books for 'Finest summer I remember' from *A Flame in your Heart* (1986).
Philip Gross and Faber & Faber for 'The Duke of Nowhere' from *The Son of the Duke of Nowhere* (1991).
Michael Hamburger and Anvil Press Poetry for 'In Doubt' from *Collected Poems 1941 - 1994* (1995).
Sophie Hannah and Carcanet Press for 'Ticket to Staines' from *Hotels like Houses* (1996).

John Harvey and Smith/Doorstop Books for 'Chet Baker' from *Ghosts of a Chance* (1992).

Geoff Hattersley and Bloodaxe Books for 'Nobel Prize Poem' from *Don't Worry* (1994).

Jeanette Hattersley and Smith/Doorstop Books for 'One Day, Her Father' from *Time of Her Life* (1993).

Rita Ann Higgins and Bloodaxe Books for 'The Did-You-Come-Yets of the Western World' from *Sunny Side Plucked* (1996).

Donna Hilbert and Event Horizon Press for 'The Doctor Book' from *Deep Red* (1993).

Selima Hill and Bloodaxe Books for 'The Island' from *Trembling Hearts in the Bodies of Dogs* (1994).

Terrence Hirst's Estate for 'Poor Moorhen Johnny' from *The Rialto 6.*

Michael Hofmann and Faber & Faber for 'On the Beach at Thorpeness' from *Corona, Corona* (1993).

Miroslav Holub and Bloodaxe Books for 'Brief Reflection on Cats Growing in Trees', translated by Ewald Osers, from *Poems Before and After: Collected English Translations* (1990).

Michael Hulse and The Harvill Press for 'Roadworkers Picking Cherries' from *Eating Strawberries in the Necropolis* (1991).

M. C. Jabber for an extract from 'Project'.

Kathleen Jamie for 'St Bride's'.

Nigel Jenkins and Gomer Press for 'Castration' from *Acts of Union: Selected Poems 1974 - 1989* (1990).

Elizabeth Jennings and Carcanet Press for 'A Classroom' from *Collected Poems* (1986).

Sylvia Kantaris and Bloodaxe Books for 'An Innocent Adultery' from *Dirty Washing* (1989).

Jaan Kaplinski and The Harvill Press for 'Death does not come from outside', translated by Hildi Hawkins, from *Through the Forest* (1996).

P. J. Kavanagh and Carcanet Press for 'News from Gloucestershire' from *Collected Poems* (1992).

Jackie Kay and Bloodaxe Books for an extract from 'The Waiting Lists' from *The Adoption Papers* (1991).

Brendan Kennelly and Bloodaxe Books for 'The Kiss' from *A Time for Voices* (1990).

Mimi Khalvati and Carcanet Press for 'I love all things in miniature' from *Entries On Light* (1997).

John Kinsella and Arc Publications for 'The Silo' from *The Undertow* (1996).

August Kleinzahler and Faber & Faber for 'Watching Young Couples with an Old Girlfriend on Sunday Morning' from *Green Sees Things in Waves* (1998).
Stephen Knight and Bloodaxe Books for 'The Surf Motel' from *Dream City Cinema* (1996).
Kenneth Koch and Carcanet Press for 'Variations on a Theme by William Carlos Williams' from *Selected Poems* (1991).
Rutger Kopland and Enitharmon Press for 'The Valley' from *A World Beyond Myself* translated by James Brockway (1991).
Frank Kuppner and Carcanet Press for 'Last Eternal Moments 13' from *Everything is Strange* (1994).
Vyacheslav Kupriyanov and Forest Books for 'Report on an Angel' from *In Anyone's Tongue* translated by Francis Jones (1992).
Ivan V. Lalíc's Estate and Anvil Press Poetry for 'Places We Love' from *A Rusty Needle* translated by Francis Jones (1996).
John Latham and Peterloo Poets for 'Change of State' from *Unpacking Mr. Jones* (1982).
Tom Leonard and Galloping Dog Press for 'Unrelated Incidents: (3)' from *Intimate Voices 1965-1983* (1984).
Gwyneth Lewis and Bloodaxe Books for 'Six Poems on Nothing: IV' from *Parables & Faxes* (1995).
Grevel Lindop and Carcanet Press for 'Summer Pudding' from *Tourists* (1987).
Liz Lochhead and Penguin Books for 'Kidspoem/Bairnsang' from *Penguin Modern Poets: Volume 4* (1995).
Christopher Logue and Faber & Faber for an extract from 'New Numbers' from *Selected Poems* (1996).
Herbert Lomas and Sinclair-Stevenson for 'Sea Lady' from *Trouble* (1992).
Michael Longley and Cape Poetry for 'The Butchers' from *Selected Poems* (1998).
John Lucas and Peterloo Poets for 'Studying Grosz on the Bus' from *Studying Grosz on the Bus* (1989).
John Lynch for 'Changes' from *Smiths Knoll 18.*
Thomas Lynch and Cape Poetry for 'Skating with Heather Grace' from *Grimalkin* (1994).
John Lyons and Smith/Doorstop Books for 'Breaking Siesta' from *Behind the Carnival* (1994).
Michael Mackmin for 'Midnight Garden' from *The Rialto 30.*
Sorley MacLean's Estate and Carcanet Press for 'Going Westwards' from *From Wood to Ridge*, translated by the author (1991).

Wes Magee and Cambridge University Press for 'Jumping Jack' from *Morning Break* (1989).
Jack Mapanje and Heinemann Educational Publishers for 'Scrubbing the Furious Walls of Mikuyu' from *The Chattering Wagtails of Mikuyu Prison* (1993).
E. A. Markham and Anvil Press Poetry for 'The Sea' from *Human Rites* (1984).
Gerda Mayer and Iron Press for 'Make Believe' from *Bernini's Cat* (1999).
Rhona McAdam and Slow Dancer Press for 'The Boston School of Cooking Cookbook' from *Old Habits* (1993).
Roger McGough and Penguin Books for 'Cinders' from *Defying Gravity* (1993).
Jamie McKendrick and Oxford University Press for 'The Marble Fly' from *The Marble Fly* (1997).
Christine McNeill and Bloodaxe Books for 'Geography Lesson' from *Kissing the Night* (1993).
Paula Meehan and The Gallery Press for 'Would You Jump Into My Grave As Quick?' from *Pillow Talk* (1994).
Hilary Mellon for 'Road Through Northern Landscape'.
Adrian Mitchell and Bloodaxe Books for 'A Puppy Called Puberty' from *Blue Coffee* (1996).
Elma Mitchell and Peterloo Poets for 'This Poem...' from *People Etcetera* (1987).
John Mole and Secker & Warburg for 'Alice and Alice' from *In And Out Of The Apple* (1984).
John Montague and The Gallery Press for 'All Legendary Obstacles' from *New Selected Poems* (1990).
Edwin Morgan and Carcanet Press for 'The First Men On Mercury' from *Poems Of Thirty Years* (1982).
Les Murray and Carcanet Press for 'It Allows a Portrait in Line Scan at Fifteen' from *Subhuman Redneck Poems* (1996).
Dorothy Nimmo and Smith/Doorstop Books for 'Moggy at Grimma's' from *The Children's Game* (1998).
Sean O'Brien and Oxford University Press for 'HMS Glasshouse' from *HMS Glasshouse* (1991).
Bernard O'Donoghue and Chatto & Windus for 'A Noted Judge of Horses' from *The Weakness* (1991).
Dennis O'Driscoll and Anvil Press Poetry for 'Way of Life' from *Long Story Short* (1993).
Sharon Olds and Alfred A. Knopf Inc. for 'The Blue Dress' from *The Sign of Saturn* (Secker & Warburg 1991).

Don Paterson and Faber & Faber for 'The Ferryman's Arms' from *Nil Nil* (1993).

Brian Patten and Harper Collins for 'A Blade of Grass' from *Vanishing Trick* (1976).

Meg Peacocke and Peterloo Poets for 'Tango' from *Selves* (1995).

Patricia Pogson and Flambard Press for 'Life' from *The Tides In The Basin* (1994).

Sheenagh Pugh and Seren for 'The Last Wolf in Scotland' from *Sing for the Taxman* (1993).

Zsuzsa Rakovszky and Oxford University Press for 'Waiting-Room' from *New Life* translated by George Szirtes (1994).

Deryn Rees-Jones and Seren for 'Lovesong to Captain James T. Kirk' from *The Memory Tray* (1994).

Mark Roper and Peterloo Poets for 'Cleaning Ladies' from *The Hen Ark* (1990).

Michael Rosen and Harper Collins for 'Hot Food' from *The Hypnotiser* (1990).

Anne Rouse and Bloodaxe Books for 'Sacrificial Wolf' from *Sunset Grill* (1993).

Tadeusz Różewicz and Anvil Press Poetry for 'Busy with Many Jobs' from *They Came To See A Poet: Selected Poems* translated by Adam Czerniawski (1991).

Carol Rumens and Bloodaxe Books for Part 6 of 'A Meeting of Innocents' from *Thinking of Skins: New & Selected Poems* (1993).

Peter Sansom and Carcanet Press for 'A Dream Mistaking a Person for What He Has Come to Represent' from *January* (1994).

Carole Satyamurti and Oxford University Press for 'Broken Moon' from *Broken Moon* (1987).

Vernon Scannell and Robson Books for 'Right Dress' from *Collected Poems 1950 -1993* (1993).

Myra Schneider and Arc Publications for 'Crossing Point' from *Crossing Point* (1991).

David Scott and Bloodaxe Books for 'Playing For England' from *Selected Poems* (1998).

Peter Scupham and Oxford University Press for 'Going out: Lancasters, 1944' from *The Air Show* (1988).

Olive Senior and McClelland & Stewart Inc., The Canadian Publishers for 'Hurricane Story, 1988' from *Gardening in the Tropics* (1995).

Jo Shapcott and Oxford University Press for 'Goat' from *Phrase Book* (1992).

Ruth Silcock and Anvil Press Poetry for 'The Elocution Lesson' from *A Wonderful View of the Sea* (1996).

Norman Silver and Faber & Faber for 'Two Boyfriends' from *Words on a Faded T-Shirt* (1991).

Charles Simic and Faber & Faber for 'Popular Mechanics' from *Frightening Toys* (1995).

Lemn Sissay for 'Flowers in the Kitchen' from *Rebel Without Applause* (Bloodaxe Books 1992).

Joan Jobe Smith and Smith/Doorstop Books for 'On the Way to Heaven' from *The Pow Wow Café* (1998).

Ken Smith and Bloodaxe Books for 'My Father Fading Out' from *The Poet Reclining* (1982).

Marin Sorescu and Bloodaxe Books for 'Omens' from *Selected Poems*, translated by Michael Hamburger (1983).

Stephen Spender's Estate and Faber & Faber for 'Dolphins' from *Dolphins* (1994).

Jean Sprackland and Spike for 'Deadnettle' from *Tattoos for Mothers Day* (1997).

Pauline Stainer for 'The Dig'.

Martin Stannard and Slow Dancer Press for 'Phil's Poem' from *The Gracing of Days* (1989).

Eira Stenberg and Bloodaxe Books for Part 1 of 'The Eighth Day of the Week' from *Wings of Hope and Daring: Selected Poems*, translated by Herbert Lomas (1992).

Anne Stevenson and Oxford University Press for 'A Prayer to Live with Real People' from *The Fiction-Makers* (1985).

Sue Stewart and Anvil Press Poetry for 'Bluebells' from *Inventing the Fishes* (1993).

Matthew Sweeney and Secker & Warburg for 'Asleep In a Chair' from *Cacti* (1992).

George Szirtes and Oxford University Press for 'A Picture of My Parents with their First Television' from *Selected Poems, 1976 - 1996* (1996).

Shuntarō Tanikawa and Carcanet Press for 'Evening' from *Selected Poems* (1998).

Grete Tartler and Oxford University Press for 'The Wonders of the World' from *Orient Express* translated by Fleur Adcock (1989).

Anthony Thwaite and Enitharmon Press for 'Cockroach Story' from *Selected Poems 1956 - 1996* (1997).

Charles Tomlinson and Oxford University Press for 'The Fox Gallery' from *The Way of a World* (1969).

Julio Valle-Castillo and Katabasis for 'Rafaela Padilla' from *The Nicaraguan Epic* translated by Dinah Livingstone (1989).
Fred Voss and Bloodaxe Books for 'Uptight' from *Goodstone* (1991).
John Wakeman for 'A Sea Family'.
Susan Wicks and Faber & Faber for 'Branches' from *Singing Underwater* (1992).
C. K. Williams and Bloodaxe Books for 'My Mother's Lips' from *New and Selected Poems* (1995).
Hugo Williams and Oxford University Press for 'When I Grow Up' from *Self-Portrait with a Slide* (1990).
Jackie Wills and Arc Publications for 'Counting' from *Powder Tower* (1995).
Frances Wilson and Rockingham Press for 'Revisiting the Pigs' from *Close to Home* (1993).
Gerard Woodward and Chatto & Windus for 'After the Deafening' from *After the Deafening* (1994).
Glyn Wright and Spike for 'Knowing Plenty' from *Could Have Been Funny* (1995).
Kit Wright and Hutchinson Press for 'Underneath the Archers' from *Bump-starting the Hearse* (1983).
Tamar Yoseloff and Slow Dancer Press for 'In the Chelsea Physic Garden' from *Sweetheart* (1998).